Hugh Chalmers

THE MILK OF THE BOSWELLIA FORESTS

Frankincense production among the pastoral Somali

The milk of the Boswellia forests

Frankincense production among the pastoral Somali

Ahmed Yusuf Farah

edited by TiiaRiitta Hjort af Ornäs

EPOS, Research Programme on Environmental Policy and Society
Department of Social and Economic Geography, Uppsala University

EPOS, Environmental Policy and Society, is an interdisciplinary research network. Its concern is environmental security in relation to competition for natural resources. *The environment and international securities*, *Local conceptual models for environmental change*, and *Environment and dryland securities* are all programmes within EPOS, based at Uppsala University. Research groups at Linköping University (*Livelihoods from resource flows*) and Stockholm (*Environment, trade and development*) are also included in the EPOS network.
Activities are financed by FRN (Swedish Council for Planning and Coordination of Research), SAREC (Swedish Agency for Research Cooperation with Developing Countries) and SIDA (Swedish International Development Authority). Anders Hjort-af-Ornäs is the Programme Director.
More information and publications can be ordered from:
EPOS, Sturegatan 9, 1 tr, S-753 14 Uppsala, SWEDEN

SAREC, the Swedish Agency for Research Cooperation with Developing Countries, receives over 3 percent of the total Swedish Government allocation for development cooperation, equalling SEK 495 million for the fiscal year 1993/94.
SAREC's task is to support research that contributes to the development of developing countries. This means, among other things
–helping developing countries to build up their own research capacity.
–supporting research which can help to solve important problems in developing countries.
–promoting scientific cooperation between Sweden and the developing countries.
More information can be received from:
SAREC, P O Box 161 40, S-103 23 Stockholm, SWEDEN
Telephone: +46 8 791 21 00   Telefax: +46 8 791 21 99   Telegram: SAREC

ISBN 91-506-1010-4

© 1994 The author and Research Programme on Environmental Policy and Society, EPOS, Department of Social and Economic Geography, Uppsala University, Sturegatan 9, 1tr, S-753 14 Uppsala, Sweden

Layout: TiiaRiitta Hjort af Ornäs
Cover photograph by the author
Cartography: Christer Krokfors and Kjerstin Andersson
Language polishing: Sharon Ford

Printed in Sweden by Reprocentralen HSC, Uppsala 1994
Cover Printed by MO Print, Uppsala 1994

Contents

List of maps, tables and figures

Maps

Tables

Figures

Map 1. *The geographical zones and frankincense-growing areas in northern Somalia*

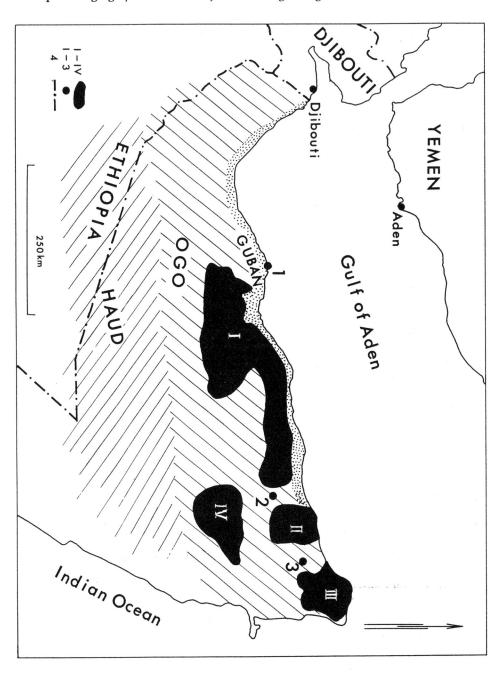

I–IV Frankincense-growing areas:
    I Cal Madow
    II Cal Miskeed
    III Cal Bari
    IV Karkar

1–3 Places mentioned in the text:
    1. Karin (West)
    2. Karin (East)
    3. Ceel-gaal

4 International boundary

Map 2. *District centres and other frankincense towns in northern Somalia*

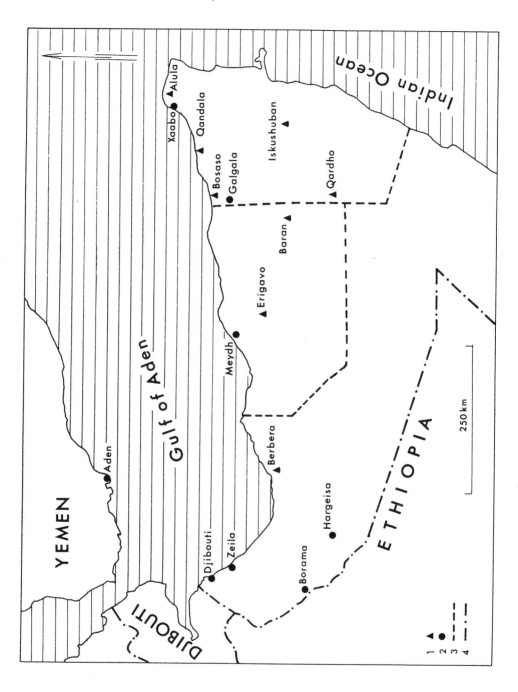

1 Administrative towns of the enterprise, and district centres
2 Towns and villages mentioned in the text
3 Boundaries of Sanaag (in the West) and Bari (in the East) regions
4 International boundary

EDITOR'S FOREWORD

The publication of the present volume was initiated in 1990 by the Somali–Swedish Somali Camel Research Project (SCRP). The president of the Somali Academy of Sciences and Arts (SOMAC) at that time, Maryan Zaarx Warsame made a request to the coordinators of the project, Mohamed Ali Hussein and Anders Hjort af Ornäs to take on the task of editing the PhD thesis of Ahmed Yusuf Farah for publication.

Although frankincense cultivation and production was not a part of the sphere of an interdisciplinary research and training project on camels, the project coordinators found the study of great interest. Ahmed Yusuf Farah was also a member of the camel research team. The present volume shows how the frankincense sector in Somalia applies a value system derived from the dominating camel culture and can only be understood in relation to this subsistence system. Therefore, seen in a wider perspective, a study on the sociology and economy of frankincense in Somalia is relevant for research on camel pastoralism.

The main purpose of this book is to present material and perspectives, practically unstudied and unpublished before. As a northern Somali himself Ahmed Yusuf Farah has deep insight in his area of study through his knowledge of the culture and language concerned. The work of the editor has therefore been to make the material as accessible as possible for a reader non-familiar with the Somali culture. The PhD thesis of the author from the London School of Economics and Political Science has been revised into the present format.

I wish to express my gratitude for their comments to Anders Hjort af Ornäs and Christer Krokfors, the former research assistant of the SCRP project. Comments on the botanical matters from Mats Thulin were greatly appreciated.

Uppsala, October 1993
TiiaRiitta Hjort af Ornäs

AUTHOR'S FOREWORD

After intermediate boarding school and secondary education, I joined Lafole College of Education in 1977. This was not because I liked the teaching profession, but mainly because it was the only college in the Somali National University that provided a two-year first degree course. I wanted to get a degree and start to work as early as possible in order to relieve the burden of education expenditure from my poor cultivating family living in Dila village near Borama town in northwest Somalia.

Of the 1979 batch of graduates, the first students in the departments of the college were exempt from teaching at high schools controlled by the Ministry of Education, and were allocated work in the administrative and research departments of the Ministry of Higher Education and Culture. I was one of the lucky graduates who were given assistant research work at the newly established Somali Academy of Sciences and Arts (SOMAC, an autonomous research institution attached to the Ministry of Higher Education) in 1980.

In 1981 the Somali Academy of Sciences and Arts and the Swedish Agency for Research Cooperation with Developing Countries (SAREC), initiated a bilateral research programme. To enhance the research capacity of the national academic institutions, SOMAC and the Somali University, the programme initiated a relatively extensive training programme for the research staff in these comparatively new institutions. I was one of the potential researchers who benefited from this generous bilateral research programme.

However, the post-graduate study of Social Anthropology at the London School of Economics and Political Science, and the doctoral work (1989) on frankincense, were not by my own deliberate choice. These were decided by officials of the SOMAC/SAREC programme. There was a frankincense project in the multi-disciplinary collaboration programme, and therefore a social anthropologist was required to undertake a socioeconomic study of the frankincense economy.

Although the field of study (1984–85) and the subject of investigation both happened by accident, it led to an interesting research career which I now greatly enjoy.

I would like to thank all the institutions and individuals who have offered their assistance on numerous occasions throughout the course of this study. I would like to make special mention of my gratitude to the sponsors of my post-graduate studies at the London School of Economics and Political Science, a bilateral research cooperation project between the Somali Academy of Sciences and Arts (SOMAC), where I am employed as research worker, and the Swedish Agency for Research Cooperation with Developing Countries (SAREC).

I wish to thank my supervisor, Mike Sallnow at the London School of Economics and Political Science, whose advice on the presentation of the data and techniques of writing an academic work have been very useful, particularly in the initial stages of the study. I would also like to express thanks to Professor I. M. Lewis for his keen interest in my post-graduate study in general and in this study in particular. His constructive comments contributed much to the improvement of the intellectual and stylistic quality of the thesis. I thank B. W. Andrzejewski for his appreciation of the anthropological analysis of frankincense sector poetry and for the extensive use of poetry throughout the thesis. He made many appropriate changes in the English translation of the Somali poems.

For their tremendous hospitality and cooperation, I thank frankincense collectors in Bari and Erigavo regions. Regional, district and local level cooperative chairmen were all very cooperative and hospitable. To mention a few, I am grateful to Xuseen Gurxan (Bosaso), Siciid Cabdikariim (Alula), Addoosh (Qandala) and Saalax Xaji Xasan (Erigavo). I would also like to thank the regional and district officials and workers of the frankincense enterprise, particularly my former secondary schoolmate, Dhuxul, who is the research director of the enterprise in the central office in Mogadishu.

I would like to thank the regional director of the customs in Bari region in 1985, Cabdi Cumar, for the substantial financial and logistic support of my field work in the frankincense-producing areas in the region. His generous support has supplemented the limited research allowance obtained from the Somali Academy of Sciences and Arts.

I am also grateful to the former presidents of the Somali Academy of Science and Arts, Cali Cabdiraxmaan Xirsi and Maryan Faarx Warsame, for their encouragement and support. My thanks go to all of my research colleagues in the Academy, particularly my friend Maxamad Xaamud Sheekh. Finally, I thank Swedish and Somali researchers in the frankincense domestication project in Somalia for their advice on the botanical literature on the plants and for the joint trips in the frankincense region during my fieldwork, A. Persson, M. Thulin and A. M. Warfa.

Last but not least I wish to express my gratitude to the EPOS (Environmental Policy and Society) research programme at Uppsala University for publishing the revised version of my thesis.

Uppsala, October 1993
Ahmed Yusuf Farah

INTRODUCTION

This study is the first anthropological work on the "ownership", production and marketing of frankincense in Somalia. It is based on ten months' field research in the northeast frankincense region of Somalia in 1984–85. The frankincense-collecting communities are sparsely distributed across a single ecological zone—the maritime escarpment which grows the frankincense-bearing species in Bari and Erigavo regions. The fairly uniform culture of these communities allows us to treat this localised but important sector of the national economy as a unit of analysis. My command of the Somali language and my intensive knowledge of the economic groups in northern Somalia, permitted me to undertake a detailed sector analysis of the subject.

Of first importance, the study is a comparative analysis of the sedentary, localised economies of frankincense gathering and crop production, within the predominant pastoral system of northern Somalia. However, the thesis has a wider comparative relevance as well. For example, the account of the development of cooperatives is a contribution to the general anthropological literature on this important topic. In the perspective of the whole study, written sources are referred to in the light of my field data.

The current uses of frankincense, both industrial and non-industrial, local and wider uses are examined in this volume. They illustrate at some length the importance of frankincense, partly because the subject is little dealt with in the literature, the sacred attributes of incense tending to obscure its other practical values.

The main focus of this study is on the commercial resin derived from two Somali Boswellia plants that grow in the northeast: yagcar and moxor. The first produces an incense that is locally known as meydi, while the latter produces beeyo. Frankincense, incense, resin, and aromatic products, are all used to refer to the products of these frankincense trees. Other commercial plant products that are obtained from widespred Commiphora plants are referred to as gums, although the particular local names of these products are commoly used. Boswellia plant products are technically described as gum-resin, nevertheless since these products are odoriferous I refer to them as incense, frankincense etc. in a general sense, but not in a technical sense.

It is impossible to understand the status of frankincense and the people involved in its production and trade without looking at the common property categories in Somalia. These are therefore dealt with early in this study. Although a limited account of the primary community resources in the northern region is given in the work of Lewis (1961) a comparative analysis of basic property categories has not previously been carried out. The dominance of the pastoral outlook and world view of the Somalis regardless of economic specialisation is a recognised predisposition but has not been adequately documented before. Somalis classify property into two broad categories: animate or pastoral wealth, nool, and inanimate or non-pastoral wealth, mood. The tenacity of pastoral values is further illustrated as the northern sedentary groups are shown to refer to a camel economic standard. In the glorification of their respective economies, rival community poet spokesmen derive metaphors and images from the

1

dominant pastoral culture. Thus frankincense collectors and sedentary cultivators in northern Somalia describe their primary sources of exploitation to be as important as camel herds.

Pastoral and sedentary landuse systems, previously described by Lewis (1961b) are compared with the frankincense tenurial pattern. I show new ethnographic material on the system of land use in the frankincense region of Somalia. Rental and share-cropping arrangements which are common in the exploitation of frankincense display unbalanced relations with respect to access to property among landless tenants and right-holders, groups who commonly belong to the same corporate lineage. These unbalanced relations regulating access to the community property are not found in other more egalitarian economic groups in northern Somalia.

These arrangements bring us to the very organisation of the frankincense production. The chief unit of production is commonly an agnatic work party whose members co-labour in a particular season. They share the investment expenditure on an equal basis. This collective rule in the sphere of production is distinguished from the consumption domain where members are individually held responsible for the seasonal credits incurred by their households. Each individual pays family credits with his respective share from the final collective proceeds, which are equally distributed after the total collective expenditure is deducted. In the past, these different economic patterns took place in a social context of exploitation between traders who were the source of credits and kin client producers. Agnatic solidarity is also very common in other economies in the north, but these are formally organised for particular purposes of collective interest. The cultivating nuclear or herding family is generally the chief unit of production and consumption.

In the last part of the study I account for the persistent failure of cooperative development in the frankincense sector in Somalia. My analysis differs from the conventional theories which claim social organisation of underdeveloped societies as the facilitating or constraining factor in the development of an effective cooperative movement. I argue that economic differences and unbalanced relations between local traders and their kin client collectors were the main dysfunctional force that hampers the cooperative movement.

CHAPTER ONE

Frankincense for trade

The Somali geography of frankincense production

As a biblical product of ancient ritual use, frankincense may be thought to be a thing of the past which has little or no significance in modern times. In Somalia, however, the natural gum industry producing frankincense is officially the third most important source of foreign exchange through exports, after livestock and bananas. Officials of the Frankincense and Gums Development and Sales Agency reasonably estimate the number of families which primarily depend upon incense gathering to be about 10,000 families. With the exception of under exploited marine resources, the frankincense region in the northern part of the country, is short of exploitable resources, such as adequate pasturage and potential agricultural land. Therefore, the occurrence of commercial frankincense forests, which is the most important sector in the natural gums industry, is crucial in terms of being a major source of subsistence for a large number of the regional population.

The narrow torrid coastal strip (Guban, from the verb *gub*, to burn) in northern Somalia contains the trading towns and small fishing communities which are engaged in exporting frankincense and other local products. Behind the low coastal belt lies the highland area (Ogo) where the commercial frankincense is produced, particularly in the maritime escarpment. The deep wells used by pastoralists are also situated in this ecological zone. The interior plateau (Haud) is chiefly a pastoral region where nomadic clans congregate during the rainy season.

In addition to frankincense, inhabitants in the northeast region attribute two non-frankincense benefits to their superficially precarious mountain region. In the past the rugged terrain acted as a safe refuge from invasion. When the interior pasture drastically diminishes and fails its inhabitants, the mountain is said to retain some left-over tufts and permanent streams that ensure the survival, if not prosperity, of stock and people. In good years of plenty, the interior plateau of Haud offers abundant pasturage and water in relation to the mountain habitat. Hence interior nomads enjoy a prosperous life that is envied by the residents in the upland, who say, however, that they prefer the security of the austere lifestyle in their country.

Frankincense people divide the maritime incense-growing range into three zones: (1) *Cal Madow*: literally "the black escarpment", the westerly extension of the escarpment which runs parallel to the coast and grows frankincense-bearing species. This westerly segment starts from Karin village east of Berbera and stretches as far as Karin village in Bosaso district; (2) *Cal Miskeed*, the middle segment of the frankincense-growing escarpment, which extends from Karin village in Bosaso towards the east as far as Ceel-gaal village in Qandala district; (3) *Cal Bari*: literally the "eastern escarpment", the eastern fringe of the frankincense-growing escarpment lying east of Cal-miskeed. Besides these areas, frankincense is also produced in the Karkar area between Qardho and Iskushuban (see Map 1).

The division of the frankincense territory to a great extent also corresponds to the social distribution of the frankincense-owning groups. But the social distribution over space is not the only criterion for the local demarcation of the frankincense mountain region. The three areas are also physiographic areas, easily divided on the basis of topographic features. Differences in these areas are also thought to affect the colour of the frankincense crop. Frankincense that is collected in the west of the escarpment is claimed to be slightly redder than the white frankincense that is produced on the eastern fringe.

Northern Somalis go further than the general tendency which customarily associates social units with particular territories. To a considerable extent, clan territories are mapped out into distinct areas. In reference to ubiquitous names which refer to prominent features that occur in their country, northern Somalis can more or less accurately describe any location in a particular area.

Frankincense fields which mostly lie in vast expanses of rugged and rocky mountain terrain understandably defy precise demarcation such as that which is found in the northwest region. Such limitation is compensated by giving names to particular frankincense fields, and also by delimiting their boundaries by means of terrestrial signs.

Major types of frankincense and their source

The trees producing both frankincense and myrrh belong to the family Burseraceae. One of the distinguishing features of the family is the presence of resin ducts in the bark. Frankincense is resin obtained from trees of the genus Boswellia, and myrrh is resin from trees of the genus Commiphora. Boswellia and Commiphora are tropical genera with concentrations of species in northeast Africa. Various species of economic importance are found in southern Arabia as well as in India and the northeastern part of Africa.

In Somalia frankincense trees grow in the northern and northeastern regions. According to Thulin and Warfa (1987) only two frankincense-producing species are found in Somalia. These are 1)Boswellia sacra (syn. B. carteri), with the Somali name *moxor*, which yields an incense which is locally known as *beeyo* and as Somali type olibanum in the international trade jargon; and 2)Boswellia frereana, with the Somali name *yagcar*, which produces an incense known as *meydi* in Somalia, and *luban lami* in Arabia. It is a localised species found only in the frankincense region of Somalia.

Besides in Somalia, B. sacra also grows in southern Arabia (Hadhramaut region in southern Yemen and Dhofar in Oman) where it has been exploited since antiquity. Frankincense derived from other species of Boswellia and referred to as Ogaden quality in international trade is also produced in the Ogaden region in Ethiopia.

The ground distribution of the *yagcar* species is characteristically described as between 5 and 60 km from the coast, while its upward distribution extends from an elevation starting from near sea level to 750 m or more (Thulin and Warfa 1987).

The *moxor* region is much more widespread than that of the maritime *yagcar*. It extends from the coastal hills to about 200 km in the hinterland. In places where the coastline is steep and rocky, it can be found growing at sea level. The highest elevation where *moxor* trees have been found growing is 1,230 m.

Apart from Somalia (and southern Arabia where small quantities of frankincense are produced mainly for domestic use), Ethiopia, Sudan and India rank as important incense-producing countries. Ethiopia and Sudan produce frankincense which is internationally referred to as Eritrean type olibanum and is derived from Boswellia papyrifera. In the arid region in northwest India Boswellia serrata is a source of comparatively inferior frankincense.

In addition to the frankincense trees, numerous species of Commiphora are also found in Somalia. Myrrh is the resin from the *dhidin* tree, Commiphora myrrha (Nees) Engl. In Somali myrrh gum is known as *malmal*. Opopanax *xabag xadi* or scented myrrh is another important gum obtained from Commiphora guidottii (Thulin and Claeson 1991).

Frankincense-producing species grow in territorially-bounded collection areas, *xiji*, which are considered locally as fields. Characteristically they belong to a core of agnatic families, most commonly less than ten nuclear families, which own one or more incense fields inherited from the first ancestor holder from whom they trace descent over one to three generations.

In contrast, the myrrh tree is very widely distributed, mainly in the dry inland areas, from Erigavo district in the north to the lower Juba in the south, with concentrations in areas closer to the Ethiopian and Kenyan borders. Important areas of collection include Laas-caanood, Gaalkacaya, Dhuusamareeb, Bakool, Gedo, Xudur, Luuq, and Baydhaba. Since large quantities of Commiphora gums are produced across the border in neighbouring Ogaden and Wajir districts in Ethiopia and Kenya, respectively, a considerable trans-border trade operates. Some sources suggest that more than half of the myrrh exports from Somalia originate in Ogaden in eastern Ethiopia (Coulter 1987:25).

Two types of myrrh distinguished by method of producing are produced. *Hussul* is superior, and larger pieces of gum and its collection by natural exudation that occurs when trees burst open after adequate rain. The gum that is harvested after scarification of the bark of the myrrh plant is known as *zara*.

In the beginning of this century, Drake-Brockman (1912:302–305) distinguished two types of myrrh. An inferior quality known as *guban malmal*, collected in the torrid coastal belt Guban, and a better quality called *ogo malmal*, gathered in the interior Ogo. At present myrrh is not produced in the northeastern frankincense region of Somalia although it is acknowledged to have been collected there in the past.

Although myrrh trees are exploited in the same manner as frankincense plants, they are not subject to such prescriptive rights as the more valuable Boswellias. Like pasturage and naturally-occurring water, access to the exploitation of Commiphora plants is not restricted. Consequently, free access and part-time exploitation by nomadic families are causing considerable damage to the trees. Less concern for impurities and sometimes adulterating species may lower the quality of the product.

As valuable export commodities, myrrh and other Commiphora gums are known to have been produced in Somalia together with frankincense for centuries. This makes it difficult to explain the sharp distinction in the rights of "ownership" of frankincense and <u>Commiphora</u> properties. Commercial frankincense is localised and produced only in the northeastern frankincense region. At present it is also more expensive than all the other natural gums that are widely distributed. Scarcity and value factors may explain the "ownership" of frankincense at present. In the past, however, the relative value of frankincense and myrrh was not as different as it is today. Presumably the demand for frankincense may have been stable over time compared to myrrh and other <u>Commiphora</u> gums.

Frankincense trade to Aden

The importance of the frankincense trade in the history of the whole Somali nation can hardly be overestimated. According to the Somali historian A. A. Hersi, the northeastern coast of Somaliland derived its importance from the ancient trade of incense goods. Myrrh and frankincense were produced substantially in southern Arabia and the Gulf of Aden maritime coastal region of northeastern Somalia. Valued for their medicinal properties, pleasant odour and sacred religious utility, gums and resins of Somaliland were exported since ancient times to classical civilisations, the Egyptians, the Assyrians, the Persians and Macedonians. To acquire these esteemed aromatic forest products ancient peoples of these civilisations were reported to pay high prices and even periodically organised fabulous expeditions to reach these exotic goods in their original sources, southern Arabia and the Horn of Africa (Hersi 1977:44–46).

The frankincense trade is not only of importance for students of Somali history and culture, but it also stimulates nostalgic feelings among Somalis, particularly the inhabitants of the geographical frankincense region, who because of the geographical location of their country are known as "the people in the east", *reer bari*. A famous elder and poet, X. Adan Afqalooc, who belongs to a frankincense-holding clan in Erigavo region, commented on the historical importance of the frankincense trade in the opening remarks of a long poem which details the Somali culture in 1983 (see Appendix, poem l))[1].

> Centuries past in the ancient history of the nation
> The time we were known as the "land of punt" and prosperity
> The Egyptian pharaohs were world power
> They purchased ostrich feathers and our *meydi* incense
> No commerce preceded the trade in frankincense merchandise
> We pioneered the mercantile craft unknown to humanity
> From those early times to the present mobile nomadic tradition of the society
> I haven't changed the traditional culture which I preach and sustain. (1)

The elder poet rightly claimed that the predominantly pastoral Somalis boast of an early mercantile culture. As the verse indicates, Somalis tend to be interested in accounts of the pharaonic Queen Hatesepsheut's fabulous expedition to the Horn of Africa in the 15th century B. C.

Ethnocentric but innocuous remarks claiming that Somalis pioneered the mercantile tradition are typical of the Somali poets who glamorise any legitimate cause at their disposal, as in this case, the glorification of the early incense trade.

---

[1] All the original Somali texts of the translated poems are presented in the Appendix.

The most longstanding and consequential of Somalia's ties with the outside world is considered to be that with Arabia. Trade networks connected coastal export centres and various inland trade routes, and the existence of many words of Arabic provenance connected to commerce in the Somali language (e.g. such basic words as trader, profit, loss, debt , loan etc.) testify to the historical trade relationships.

In modern times, from the 19th century until after the Second World War, Aden was the major export emporium for Somali gums (see Groom 1981, for the frankincense trade). Merchants there processed and re-graded imported incense for export to the international consumers.

Following the occupation of Aden by the British in 1839 as a stopping point on the short route to India, a parallel livestock trade to Aden also became very important (cf. Lewis 1980:40). This trade substantially increased to the extent that in 1869 the northern Somali port of Berbera supplied all the livestock consumed by the British garrison there and other inhabitants of Aden (cf. Swift 1979:448–449). Exported live animals and indeed frankincense merchandise were exchanged for imported grain, sugar, dates, iron, beads, salt and especially cloth from America and India.

Using oral sources obtained from the elders in the northeast frankincense region, the following account is a reconstruction of the unbalanced frankincense trade relations Somali merchants claim they experienced in Aden. Somali informants speak of oppression meted out against them by Arab patrons in the beginning of the twentieth century. At this time an increasing number of local Yemenis joined the flourishing business in Aden which had earlier been dominated by Europeans, Indians and other outsiders.[2]

My account refers to the period from early twentieth century until 1977 when the Somali government severed diplomatic ties with the Yemen Democratic Republic because of its support to Ethiopia in the 1977–78 Ogaden War. I realise that the data is a one-sided construction and tells us almost nothing about mercantile culture and specialisation in Aden at the time, and may also have a limited historical value. However, given these limitations, I hope it will generate some useful information which may enable us to compare the terms of trade that existed in Aden, with the well-documented relations that operated between foreign merchants and Somali patrons in the major trading centres in Somalia.

Incense men in Erigavo district marked the closing of the incense harvesting season by this song which they sang, and still sing, when the goods are being finally packaged for transportation to major collection centres.

I and incense are tired of each other
It is time that you (incense) move on to town stores and trading dhows
From the coastal export towns men escorted a blessing to the exported incense. (2)

So that the white and stocky Arabs may not defer your sale
May Allah make them relish you the way they cherish amber. (3)

---

[2] For details of the trade between Aden and northern Somalia, see Gavin 1975.

Written sources indicate that marketing conditions for frankincense were disadvantageous in Aden. Somalis were often forced to sell frankincense at knock-down prices. In the absence of special stores, delay in selling fragile frankincense goods caused deterioration in the quality of the product and consequent price reduction (cf. Lawrie 1954:26).

Elders in the frankincense region state that prior to the development of Aden as a commercial centre, frankincense was exported to the distant port of Bombay in India. Many elderly people still remember relatives lost in those hazardous journeys to Bombay. Such journeys are frequently mentioned in the Zeila *"aawi"* dance songs popular in Borama and the old city of Zeila. Captain S. B. Miles (1872:65) mentioned the frankincense trade to India and related that *meydi* incense was exported to Jedda and Yemeni ports, while *bedawi* quality which corresponds to the *beeyo* type was sent to Bombay to be re-exported to Europe.

Despite their dissatisfaction with the prevailing marketing conditions, Somalis preferred to trade in Aden. First, because of its close proximity to the Somali northern coast. Secondly, the dhows that plied between Somalia and external markets were not strong enough for distant ventures.

Notwithstanding the above-mentioned factors, the ability of many Somalis to speak Arabic and their understanding of Islamic culture in general has indeed been a promoting factor in the development of trade between Aden and the northern region of Somalia. Literacy in Arabic was not only important in dealing with Aden merchants, it was also valuable for Somali merchants in running their local shops effectively. To infuse an aura of honesty in credit accounts provided for collectors, most traders in Bosaso district added a sacred note in Arabic, reading "Of all legitimate observers God is the one ultimately trustworthy", in the individual credit accounts for clients. Traders non-literate in Arabic employed a religious man with a rudimentary knowledge of reading and writing to keep credit records and occasionally to calculate loss and profit accounts.

Today credit records of local traders do not contain sacred notes to affirm commercial honesty for gullible clients. However, most traders literate in Arabic still prefer to keep records in Arabic instead of Somali which has been written in the Latin script since 1972 and is widely used throughout the country.

Before the 1960s, when the British constructed a store to be used by Somalis in Aden, store installations were owned by non-Somalis. An assumed calculated reluctance of store owners to allow Somalis to store their goods for any length of time, and the fragile nature of frankincense which requires protection from heat and moisture, is said to have impelled Somalis to sell their goods promptly for knock-down prices, without market speculation.

Escorted by Somali brokers resident in Aden, Somalis approached Arab merchants. It is reported that they were not uncommonly subjected to degradation. For instance, a sales promotion call at the home of an Arab merchant is reported to have sometimes earned Somalis a hurled insult, often by children. In some cases, a knock on the door was deliberately ignored.

From the beginning of the twentieth century, Yemeni nationals in Aden may have monopolised the trade in frankincense because of awareness of or intimate knowledge of types of commercial frankincense, since a small quantity of frankincense has been produced in southern Yemen.

Some Somalis may have had regular patrons, but I was not able to obtain from the Somali informants the terms used to describe this relation, although, as will be seen shortly, patron-client relationship between small-scale Somali traders in Aden and their kin clients did have a derogatory term.

Those Yemeni merchants who favoured Somalis by agreeing to buy their goods, usually obliged them to transport the goods to the trade store. Sometimes the purchase was not effected immediately and had to wait on the convenience of the patron. This was seen as a ruthless tactic to reduce expectations and force the Somali customer to accept arbitrary low price. Moreover, in the event of purchase, frankincense packed in jute sacks or some other containers was slashed in the middle with a knife, ostensibly to display the goods for observation on the floor of the store. The customer not satisfied with the transaction was not in a position to terminate it, since his container had been damaged and goods spilled over the floor of the store.

Apart from the official duties, Aden merchants levied special payments upon their Somali clients. The most important tribute was known as *berberi* (derived from the northern port of Berbera) which amounted to 12.5 kg of free incense for every 100 kg bought from the Somali customer. Another form of expedited free incense, *raajicad*, which differs from the former in amount was also exacted by Yemeni merchants in Aden. This is reported to have amounted to 6 kg of unpaid incense for a certain amount of purchased incense.

The service of the merchant staff also counted against Somalis who were in a subordinate position to Arabs working in the store. It is said that the accountant was able to fiddle the sale price and hence deceive the vulnerable Somali. Similarly the sale's conductor was also able to hold back the weighing scale surreptitiously in order to extort extra unaccounted incense in the process.

Not infrequently, many Somalis were required to exchange the value of their goods in unpaid cash price for consumer items available at the time in the store of an Arab merchant. Although cash payments were not impossible, especially after the Second World War, and anyhow Somalis desired most of the exchange goods on offer, the barter practice denied some Somalis the choice to shop for suitable or worthy goods. In some cases, Arab merchants demanded that incense be exchanged for shoddy goods that might have expired or remained in store for a long time, such as rice spoiled by water or low quality cloth. Thus Somalis acted as a dumping ground for undesirable products that Arabs were keen to clear out.

Another mechanism used to swindle the Somali merchant, involved making heavier weights that gave a false value favourable to the Arab purchaser. Because of these problems Somalis found it imperative to arrange terms with merchant staff, usually by paying tips to avert the consequences of their deceptive tendencies.

Backdating cheques, or making them payable to an Arab crony who might demand or persuade the Somali to exchange the value of the cheque for goods in his store has also been reported to have occurred in many cases. Particularly interesting is a recent story told by a cooperative accountant in Erigavo. An Arab merchant who bought his frankincense in Aden in 1966 went to Egypt without settling accounts with his Somali client. After two months waiting for him to return, the Somali finally returned home. The indebted Arab fortunately came to Somalia to get frankincense in 1976. Anticipating the reprisal of the Somali, he remitted the standing debt to the regional account of the Somali shortly before his trip to the frankincense region of Somalia.

Somalis claim some sort of understanding existed between Aden merchants to maintain their superior position vis-à-vis Somali traders. For example, if a Somali was dissatisfied with a particular transaction, and hence tried to change to a different patron, he was rebuffed or told to return to the first dealer or else be subjected to worse treatment.

After the 1950s most of the special tributes ceased and the scale of exploitation greatly diminished. Nothwithstanding the British-constructed store mentioned earlier which did improve the situation, a small-scale Somali community emerged in Aden as a result of the frankincense and livestock trade before independence. Some of the Somalis living in Aden started as brokers mediating between Arabs and their kin traders from areas of their origin in Somalia.

Certainly Somalis preferred to trade with their kin traders in Aden. They could use the customary kin obligation to try to reduce exploitation, haggle over price, and moreover demand credits and other forms of assistance. Besides this, Somali traders were given a derogatory term, *dooxato* , literally "rippers". This refers to the practice mentioned earlier where incense packages were slashed in the middle to pour the contents on the floor of the store for observation and evaluation, a practice detested by the Somalis.

At this point it may be of interest to note the position of the Somali brokers in Aden. With respect to kin obligations, they were expected to assist in getting satisfactory value for the Somali products from Arabs whom they were powerless against. Since it was in their interest to sell the goods to obtain a commission, they had to try to convince kin owners, not satisfied with a deal, to accept it.

The broker's persuasion and the owner's reluctance to accept a deal, sometimes developed into a heated argument if not a small scuffle. Hence Somalis vented anger and frustration against their kin brokers which might not be levelled against the powerful Arab merchants directly. We may say they were caught between conflicting forces, that is their desire to maintain the system which was their subsistence means and the moral assistance to their kin traders which they were not in a position to carry out satisfactorily.[3]

Writing on the relevance of the lineage organisation for modern commerce in northern Somalia, I. M. Lewis (1962b) rightly argued that in northern Somalia, extensive political and economic links between the urban and rural society transpose the ties of agnatic solidarity on town life and in the sphere of commerce. Trade and trading villages are considered an integral part of the corporate interest of the lineage's, and therefore must be promoted by using the pervasive idiom of agnation which serves as the foundation of collective interest.

Each lineage produces its rural entrepreneurs who seasonally or permanently operate retail and coffee shops that serve tea in the smaller rural villages in the territory that is customarily associated with the group and generally dominated by its members. As Lewis explained, success in trade by individual members is considered in terms of the general well-being of the lineage and, I may say, is valued as a source of pride in the intra-lineage competition for honour and excellence.

---

[3] In chapter four we will see how local traders employed some mechanisms of exploitation similar to those existing in Aden against their kin collectors in the frankincense-producing areas in Somalia.

Traders and townspeople consider it a legitimate right to obtain the protection and support of their *"dia*-paying group" which they are also customarily subject to patronise.[4]

Institutions to organise long distance trade in the Horn, inhabited by traditionally warring and antagonistic clans, appeared very early in history. To bring the goods produced for trade in the hinterland to northern coastal export towns, proprietors of the Somali camel caravan trade entered into a relationship of protection (trade patronage or *abbaan*) with prominent members of the hostile clans through whose territory they passed (cf. Lewis 1962b:380–381).

Gifts, wages or both, and sometimes a share in the profit, paid to the Somali patron, and the belief that a treaty entered into in good faith ought to be binding for both parties, effectively extended the full protection of the *abbaan's* lineage to foreign traders. As Lewis explained, it was the duty of the protecting lineage to avenge and demand full compensation for any damages inflicted on the caravan by another lineage. Somali *abbaans* also looked after the general interest of foreign merchants and furthermore acted as "agents", "brokers", or "caretakers", maintaining order among the Somali customers in the northern coastal towns (*ibid.* 381).

Despite isolated instances of reported extortion exacted by some Somali *abbaans* from foreign traders, perhaps the most significant effect of the trade patronage for the Arab and Indian merchants who earlier dominated the export trade in the major trading towns was the rigidity of the institution. Swift has suggested that the position of the *abbaan* was hereditary and not transferable (cf. 1979:450). Consequently, a foreign trader dissatisfied with the performance or integrity of the Somali *abbaan* was not able to terminate the relationship.

Since foreign merchants seeking protection considered membership of a prominent social group and some positive qualities of the *abbaan* , it is unlikely that many of them ended up in dealing with difficult Somali protectors. Albeit being introduced into the exclusive Somali clan system, it seems that foreign traders were sympathetically and honestly treated by northern Somalis. Whether we consider this a lack of sophistication or a Somali character seeing foreigners as weak individuals without clan affiliation and therefore deserving protection, their apparently benign treatment sharply contrasts with the oppression Somalis claim to have been subjected to in Aden.

Production and marketing policies

Relations of economic exploitation seem to have obtained persistently between incense collectors and local merchants. Understandably this has provided a moral justification for governments to intervene in the sector, often in the establishment less exploitative marketing organisations.

Written sources indicate that during the period of colonial rule, prior to independence in 1960, the Italians tried to introduce changes in the marketing of frankincense. In 1930, the then Italian governor in Bosaso introduced a marketing policy which ruled that goods must be sold at auction in local markets (cf. Guidotti 1930:10). Collectors in Baargaal village enthusiastically

---

[4] See chapter two for further details of the importance of lineage in commerce and the social organisation of the Somali.

welcomed the change as witnessed by a poem composed to celebrate the event[5] and lauding the benign colonial governor and his policy. An enterprise known as "Olibanum Incorporation" was established to improve marketing conditions. Unfortunately events in the Second World War caused the enterprise to fail.

Consequently, the trade relapsed into the hands of local merchants who dominated until 1948. In that year, according to an expatriate marketing report prepared for the civilian government preceding the present revolutionary regime, multinational enterprises (Seferian, Besse) developed an interest in the trade and tried to introduce an effective marketing organisation (cf. Henrikson 1968:22).

After a brief unsuccessful involvement, the multinational companies ceased their activities in Somalia in 1951. Henrikson explains their failure as primarily due to the tenacity of the customary bond between the local incense collectors and their kin traders who were the source of essential credits. Hence the trade once more was taken over by local traders.

With financial assistance from the Credito Somalo Bank, during the colonial period, a cooperative experiment was initiated in the frankincense-producing districts in Bosaso region. A consortium known as "Consorsio Incenso Migiurtinia Somalo" (CIMS) was founded in 1955. Like its predecessors, this cooperative scheme of change collapsed in 1958 (*ibid.*:23).

In the British Somaliland protectorate, the colonial administration's policy for the contiguous frankincense region, Erigavo, had been modest compared to the interventionist policy of the Italian administration pursued in Bosaso region. The British, however, were not indifferent to the oppressive marketing system for the poor collectors, and considered the possibility of introducing public auctions in Aden for the frankincense imported from Somalia. The idea was later dropped, thus opting not to interfere in marketing principles as testified in an unpublished report (Peck 1937). Before independence in 1960, the British built a much-needed warehouse to be used by Somalis in Aden, and another store in Meydh village in Erigavo district. Somali merchants from Bosaso region under the Italian rule knew this store as the "northern store". Northern Somalis in the Somaliland protectorate were—and still are—known as "northerners" by southern Somalis.

Apparently not reflecting on the past colonial experience in Bari region, the independent Somali civilian government which succeeded colonial rule, adopted a similar strategy that sought to create effective marketing organisations and aimed among other things, to eliminate or reduce exploitation of frankincense collectors. A government enterprise, Entente Nationale Ammassi Motoaratura (ENAM) was set up. This parastatal organisation collapsed in 1963 as the previous marketing bodies in the colonial era had done. (cf. Henrikson 1968:25).

On March 30, 1965 a decree was issued celebrating the institution of a public organisation named Ente Nazionale Incenso (ENI). The organisation started to function before the parliament had approved it, and eventually ceased operating for lack of parliamentary authorisation (*ibid.*:25).

Henrikson summarised the reasons for the frankincense sector's resistance to modernisation and change as follows: Quoting a 1965 FAO report prepared for the Somali government, he indicted bad management, problems of quality and

---

[5] See chapter seven.

quantity of the goods, lack of qualified workers to adequately perform grading and sorting, and overmanning of the marketing organisations. The agents of reform often failed to disrupt the traditional relations between the client incense collectors and their merchant kin. Also they had not been able to provide credit and other services more desirable than those provided by the local merchants. The monopoly often led to an informal market, and collectors found it profitable to sell superior frankincense for higher prices to the private traders rather than to the public organisation which paid lower prices. The collectors sold unattractive inferior merchandise for the regulated price to the introduced organisations. The collectors claimed not to have become accustomed to a cashe conomy and therefore defaulted or delayed paying credits to Credito Somalo Bank. Local state agents were not capable carrying out rational economic decisions, since important decisions were taken at higher levels. Decentralised administration encouraged embezzlement and fraud.

The most important single factor restraining the development of an effective enterprise in the frankincense sector of Somalia is the exploitation of frankincense collectors by local kin merchants. I think other dysfunctional factors should be considered only as supplementary forces which contribute to undermine the development of a viable and dynamic enterprise. This pattern of kinship exploitation was already seen in the trade to Arabia and it will be even more evident as we look at the cooperative enterprises.

From 1971 the revolutionary government that came to power in 1969 organised frankincense collectors into local cooperatives. The frankincense sector became a specialised department in the National Trade Agency, which had been created to handle imports and exports except livestock for which a separate organisation, the Livestock Development Agency had been established.

The frankincense enterprise which was set up to reform and modernise the traditional sector was placed under the sphere of the Union of the Somali Cooperative Movement (USCM) in 1984, because of stated privatisation policy, following the disappointing performance of the public organisations in general. Hence the enterprise took the title, Frankincense and Gums Development and Sales Agency. This organisation like its predecessors is the only one officially permitted to export frankincense, although private traders are allowed to export Commiphora gums, myrrh, opopanax and inferior qualities of frankincense.

There are nine district offices in the two frankincense regions, Bari and Sanaag. Each district office has warehouse facilities for storing and processing frankincense prepared for export. However, the former government facilities are not functioning at present. Except Qardho district which is exclusively *beeyo*-producing, all the other districts process *meydi* type of incense for shipment. (See Map 2).

The organisation had five departments each with its own director. The director with the general management formed the organisation's management board. The headquarters were in Mogadishu. Exports were handled via offices in Mogadishu and Berbera, with *beeyo* and myrrh exported from the former and *meydi* from the latter.

The organisation had about 200 permanent staff, most of them working in district offices, employed as administrators, accountants, clerks, graders, storekeepers etc. A considerable number of temporary staff and manual labour were recruited at times of peak activity. Including allowances, most of the permanent staff received a salary within the range from 1,000–2,000 SoShs per month (equivalent to USD 11.1–22.2 at the time of the field study, at the official rate of exchange). This salary could barely sustain an average family living in a district town for two days. The gap between official wages and the cost of living undermined workers' commitment to government employment, and encouraged corruption and all sorts of subtle means of supplementing the meagre pay.

All important tasks in the enterprise, except administrative work, were performed in the traditional way. It is interesting to note that grading was supervised and evaluation of the purchased frankincense was done by local employees of the organisation who were recruited from Aden where they acted as brokers or small-scale traders. These introduced the system of grading in the frankincense sector of Somalia and worked in the districts of their ethnic groups. This illustrates that the most important technical duty of the organisation was still carried out by local experienced people not formally trained for the job, but who gained traditional knowledge early in their lives as collectors and acquired the technique of sorting raw goods from abroad in Aden.

Processing is manual and consists chiefly of hand picking operations, separating composite material by striking it with batons or cutting with knives. Separation of the bark is done by using a wide winnowing basket.

Sorting and grading is chiefly a women's task, though supervising men may initiate the process by sieving the raw or semi-processed incense into various sizes. The women are part-time labourers and at the time of this study earned 50 SoShs for a certain amount of task, which may take one working day for a slow or a new cleaner to complete. Besides the low pay, the job is difficult and dirty for the resin sticks to the body and skin, and the environment is smothered with incense dust the effects of which are not yet known. There are no special clothes designed to protect the worker from the sticky resin, though women wear worn out clothes and paint their faces and hands with clay which facilitates washing off the sticky resin after work. Given this difficult and unrewarding task, it is not surprising that the women are mainly daughters of poor families raising some income for their families, or widows who do not get enough support from able close kin. Only those with no alternative means may stay in the job. Those who manage to earn a small income just sufficient to start a shanty corner tea shop, a branch dominated by women, leave the task of sorting and grading frankincense.

Meydi is processed into seven commercial grades. The first four grades are exported to Arabia. These most valuable grades are packaged in jute-covered 25 kg cartons that are designed to prevent the fragile goods from getting pulverised during handling. Since *meydi* incense, particularly the first two grades *mushaad* and *mujarwal* that consist of large pieces, are very expensive, they are handled with great care. Other commercial grades of *meydi* and *beeyo* are packaged in 50 kg jute sacks. In comparison, *beeyo* tears are smaller and harder and therefore endure rough handling more than fragile *meydi* products, though rough handling may cause blocking.

Information for the analysis of processing yield, description and standards of commercial frankincense, and the quantitative data on the international trade of frankincense and <u>Commiphora</u> gums have been derived from an expatriate marketing study carried out for the Somali government. It was written by J. Coulter, a marketing specialist at the Tropical Development and Research

Institute in London in June 1987. The author visited the major consumers of gum-resins, major trading centres and the Somali frankincense regions.

Quoting local expert opinion, Coulter estimated that on average, *meydi* yields about 50% of the four most valuable grades, including 25% of *mushaad* and *mujarwal*. These figures were compared to those obtained for Erigavo in 1985 (29.4% and 12.9% respectively), and those obtained in Djibouti (70–80% and 40–45% respectively). It is also suggested that the low figures obtained in Erigavo are not unique but match those obtained in other districts where incense is processed, as well as the results of the deliveries to Berbera for the same year, 1985.

The high proportion of valuable grades noted in Djibouti is shown to contrast well with the low proportion obtained in Erigavo. This reflects a tendency for low grade material to be delivered to the official enterprise, while much of the superior grade material is traded in the informal market, something that will be discussed in detail in the last chapter.

On the basis of estimates offered by the organisation, yields provided by a storekeeper in Mogadishu, and estimates calculated by the author for dispatches from Qardho in the period between January 1985 and June 1986, yields of *beeyo*, grades 1 and 2, obtained in Qardho were 54–58%. The result is lower than the 70% given by the expert opinion, although the difference is narrower than that of *meydi*. The corresponding figures for Mogadishu varied considerably from the other sources. This led Coulter to conclude that there is no control system to permit processing yields to be checked against standards.

For <u>Commiphora</u> gums there does not exist any regular grading system. Collectors bring ungraded gums to dealers. Manual processing is mainly done in Mogadishu, to where the products produced in central Somalia are transported generally. The gums are broadly categorised as cleaned or uncleaned, selected or unselected. Superior selected myrrh is described as transparent, sticky and crystalline upon breaking; unselected inferior myrrh appears as brown, opaque and conglomerate pieces mixed with bark and other impurities.

Lack of a reliable sorting system and the practice of adulterating species in a single shipment, has been suggested by Coulter to be primarily responsible for the quality problems which are reported to occur in exports destined for Europe and China.

Handling and packaging of <u>Commiphora</u> gums is not as delicate a matter as that of *meydi* incense. Like olibanum, the gum is packaged in 75 kg jute sacks, though myrrh is thought to lose its oil content which is an important factor for its value.

Private trade is legal and common in the natural <u>Commiphora</u> gums industry. Informal handling takes place in the form of under-invoicing or outright trafficking of these gums to avoid duties and financial regulations. In the case of frankincense, particularly the expensive *meydi* incense, the first commercial grades are mostly exported illicitly.

Coulter described three driving forces for the pervasive informal market: (1) The great difference between the official and informal exchange rates. He estimated that an illegal exporter can obtain about 150 SoShs per USD of exports, while exports through the official system, with 50% in hard currency and 50% in Shillings at the official rate of 90 SoShs, yield only 120 SoShs per USD of export; (2) A tax of 17% on FOB (free on board) value for all gum exports; and (3) The need to obtain hard currency to import customer goods which traders commonly acknowledge to profit from more than exported goods of frankincense and livestock.

Most of the illegally exported *meydi* goes to Djibouti for export to Arabia, while *beeyo* incense is exported to Aden and Djibouti. Myrrh mainly goes to Kenya and Djibouti.

Coulter stated that Somalis travelling to Saudi Arabia and Djibouti often carry with them small quantities of *meydi* as part of their personal effects. At times large quantities are carried by presumably influential individuals who are permitted to export substantial quantities despite the monopoly.

Coulter's marketing study points out the ambiguity relating to the information on the trade of *beeyo* incense. On the one hand, Somali sources designate public enterprise the chief purchaser, with small quantities falling into the hands of the private traders. On the other hand, European buyers to date obtain most of their requirement from merchants in Djibouti and Aden.

Private dealers mainly handle <u>Commiphora</u> gums although the government has long aspired to integrate it into the entirely collectivised frankincense sector. Gum collectors, mainly nomads, sell to buyers in rural villages or transport the goods to Mogadishu. In some cases the gums are smuggled across the border to neighbouring countries.

International trade

Official statistical data from the Somali frankincense sales agency is unreliable. The unrecorded but substantial parallel trade and the fact that different species may be counted as a single one in a shipment further complicate the matter. The fact that Coulter's report depends much on trade statistics may cause problems when estimating the volume of trade for particular gums, as the following paragraph indicates.

The total estimated value of USD 15.6 million for frankincense and gums annually exported from Somalia sharply contrasts with the average official figures of 2.8 million USD for Somali gum exports in 1984 and 1985, including significant quantities of gum Arabic.

As mentioned earlier, exotic *meydi* incense is exploited only in the frankincense region of Somalia. Coulter estimated the overall production at around 1,000 tonnes per annum. Export volume, including no less than 500 tonnes of valuable chewing grades, is estimated at around 800–900 tonnes. Of this about 500–600 tonnes is exported unofficially via Djibouti, and only some 215 tonnes (1983–1984) by the agency. The difference forms part of the locally traded inferior quality. Chief consumers are Saudi Arabia and other Middle Eastern countries. Exports to those countries at present mainly pass through Djibouti. On average, *meydi* incense fetches an international price which is relatively higher than that for the other gums, with prices delivered to warehouse in Djibouti ranging from USD 1.75 to 40 per kg varying with quality.

Coulter explained that demand and price for the superior chewing qualities of *meydi* have tremendously increased in oil-rich Middle Eastern countries since the early 1970s, following the oil boom. The 1986 marketing pattern for *meydi* illustrates well the relations between demand and the vigour of the oil economy. Demand has fallen, most probably due to the slump in the oil prices which adversely affected the price of the product.

The 1971 official producer prices for the two types of frankincense in Somalia were similar, 4.80 SoShs per kg for *meydi* first grade, and 4 SoShs per kg for first grade *beeyo* tears. Since then the price for *meydi* has dramatically increased, reaching 600 SoShs per kg in 1985. This substantial price increase for the expensive *meydi* incense has largely come as a result of competition for the product from the parallel market. The informal price for *meydi* has increased from 250–1,000 SoShs during the time of the study, 1984/85.

Because of the large difference between the producer price and the market value of the product, traders benefit more than the actual producers even in the informal economy. Coulter reported that Somali traders who run the parallel market obtain roughly double the price paid to the collector (900–1,000 SoShs per kg of *meydi*) in Djibouti.

Saudi Arabia is the chief market. It imports more than 80% of the total export value, with a high proportion of the most valuable chewing grades. Other significant markets are the Yemen Arab Republic and Egypt, the latter of which mainly imports inferior and cheaper commercial grades *fas-saqiir*, *shooto*, and *jimaanjim*, most of them used as burning incense. *Meydi* is a prestige product and is valued in Saudi Arabia as a social commodity which is mainly consumed by women in the household during social gatherings.

Coulter explained that customers fall into two categories. Regular customers are mainly Saudis and Yemenis resident in the country. The other group consists of periodical pilgrims including people visiting from other Arab countries for *Haj*, an obligatory pilgrimage made in accordance with the Islamic calendar, or *Umrah*, a non-obligatory pilgrimage made at any other convenient time, and who take home *meydi* as a gift *par excellence* and souvenir.

The Somali type olibanum *beeyo* is produced in large quantities in the frankincense region of Somalia and the contiguous Ogaden region. Exports from Somalia are estimated by Coulter not to exceed 150 tonnes a year, with international value of USD 40,000 (exempting those years in which ungraded *beeyo* is sold to China). The chief markets are the EEC countries where it is entirely consumed by the perfumery industry, and China where it has some medicinal uses. Current EEC imports are estimated by Coulter at about 190 tonnes per annum, with some growth in consumption. The Somali produce is now mainly sent to the EEC through Djibouti and Aden. A greater proportion of the trade in olibanum is handled by dealers based in Hamburg, Marseilles and Jedda, as well as one dealer based in Geneva.

The international price for the Somali olibanum is about USD 6 per kg C&F (cost and freight) in Europe for grade 1, and 3 dollars per kg for ungraded frankincense, although a lower price was reported for the Ogaden quality. The most widely traded olibanum is the Eritrean type. Eritrea and other parts of Ethiopia were the traditional sources of this frankincense. However, in the 1980s because of migrant refugees from Ethiopia with knowledge about the exploitation of frankincense, Sudan became the major supplier. Overall exports including informal trade are estimated by Coulter to exceed 2,000 tonnes per annum.

China, North Africa, Europe and Latin America are the major markets for the Eritrean type of olibanum. In China it is used as an ingredient in traditional pharmaceutical products, while in North African countries (Egypt, Libya, Algeria, Tunisia and Morocco), it is used as a chewing gum. In some Arab countries it is also used in traditional medicine. Mixed with water the solution is drunk by patients suffering from stomach ailments.

In Europe, the Eritrean type olibanum is mainly used in church rituals. The bulk of consumption takes place in countries with a substantial Greek orthodox Christian population, i.e. Greece, the former Yugoslavia, Turkey and Romania. Comparatively speaking, Roman Catholic churches use less incense in ritual. In Latin American countries the habit of burning incense is though more widespread, as Coulter noted. Incense is burned not only in churches, but is also offered in other rites of various types.

Coulter estimated the volume of the North African market to be in the range of 1,000 tonnes in 1984. Since then it has roughly halved due to import restrictions. The figures do not account for the informal imports into Egypt from Sudan, which are thought to be substantial. Saudi Arabia is estimated to consume 120 tonnes per annum, while European and Latin American markets are thought to absorb an estimated 500 tonnes per year. Most of China's olibanum imports (1,675 tonnes in 1984) were of the Eritrean type.

The domestic crisis of the 1970s in Ethiopia made the Eritrean type olibanum scarce and expensive. In 1981, Coulter reported that C&F prices in Hamburg reached around USD 5 per kg for white superior tears. Since then production has increased and prices decreased to a level comparatively lower than the price for the Somali type olibanum—roughly USD 1.50–2.00 per kg, depending on the quality of the product.

There is another type of frankincense of commercial importance, produced in the arid areas of northern India. It is mainly used domestically for making incense sticks. Official export statistics for the years 1978/79 were 444 tonnes. Major markets are USA, Middle Eastern countries (especially Iraq, Oman and Syria), Hong Kong and Singapore. In those periods when Eritrean olibanum became scarce, Indian olibanum became much used instead, particularly for ritual purposes. However, the fragrance of the Ethiopian olibanum is superior to that of the Indian incense, and with the recovery of production in Ethiopia, demand for the latter has declined so that in 1984/85 exports were only 179 tonnes.

Substantial quantities of Indian olibanum are reported to be exported to Dubai, where it is chiefly burned to fumigate homes. Greater quantities are said to be bought by people from Oman which itself produces a small quantity of frankincense.

Frankincense collectors, traders and enterprise officials know very little about the uses to which frankincense is put by the final consumers. The stable demand for frankincense and the tremendous price increase of some types of incense during the 1970s and early 1980s led Somalis to believe that exotic frankincense must be of crucial importance for the consumers, particularly Western countries.

Viewed by the local producers as an expert who graduated on a special course on frankincense, I was expected to answer every question on the subject during my field-study. They found it difficult to believe my explanation—that "Somali type olibanum" is chiefly used by the perfume industry in the West, and *meydi* incense as a chewing material in Saudi Arabia—because they were convinced of another kind of use of the product in the West.

One commonly perceived idea among people in the frankincense region of Somalia explaining the demand for frankincense in the West, is the role it is thought to play in the military industry. One informant suggested that it forms the explosive power of many weapons, particularly nuclear bombs. A regional militia chief in Bosaso town stressed that the fire created by exploding frankincense is not readily extinguishable. This quality explained its suitability in the manufacture of napalm bombs! Indeed, many were the stories told by inquisitive individuals concerning exploding lumps of frankincense to test its power.

Some good reasons underlie this popular belief. Frankincense balls are flammable if set on fire. People seem to believe that were it not essential for the military industry, the West would have ceased buying frankincense produced in Africa. Later I learned that such beliefs have been corroborated by unscrupulous national scholars who visited some areas in the frankincense region.

Annual world trade in <u>Commiphora</u> gums, in their turn, is estimated by Coulter to exceed 1,500 tonnes per year. At least 70% of this is myrrh (including some *hagar* or low grade myrrh), the remainder being mostly opopanax. Somalia is the main supplier of these gums, although a greater proportion of its exports are thought to originate across the border in Ogaden. Ethiopia, Kenya, Djibouti and the Peoples Democratic Republic of Yemen (PDRY) are other significant exporters. The latter two countries deal mainly with transhipped gums, and PDRY produces a small quantity of opopanax which is locally used.

China is the biggest consumer of <u>Commiphora</u> gums. It obtains them directly from suppliers in Africa or dealers in Hong Kong and Europe. Neither consumption nor the source has been stable over the years, with marked changes from year to year.

Other important markets are Europe, Saudi Arabia, India and Taiwan. In Europe the main consumer is the perfume industry, which is estimated to use 70 tonnes of myrrh and opopanax. Some of these gums have ritual use. For instance the incense that is burned in Roman Catholic churches contains myrrh.

The gums are also known to have some limited medical applications, e.g. their use in toothpaste's and mouth washes. In Saudi Arabia it is said that myrrh has the same use as olibanum. It is burned, or mixed with water as medicinal solution that is drunk. These natural forest products are mainly traded by dealers in Europe and Jedda, so that the quantities imported into these countries are often larger than the quantities actually consumed.

Coulter reported that producer prices varied between 120 and 300 SoShs depending on the purity and quality of the gum. The FOB international price per kilo in November 1986 was USD 6–7 for myrrh, USD 3.5–4 for opopanax and USD 3 for *hagar*.

Manufacturers of wholesale ingredients, with a high concentration in the south of France in the city of Grasse and its neighbours, actually process the Somali type of olibanum, and other <u>Commiphora</u> gums (myrrh and opopanax). Two types of products, essential oils and extracts (either absolutes or resinoids) are prepared by these companies for resale to the manufacturers of perfume.

Distillation of the raw gum produces essential oil. Superior quality with a higher oil content is usually preferred for this process, i.e. first grade tears being ideal in the case of olibanum. Resinoids are produced by extraction of the gum with a hydrocarbon solvent, and absolutes by extraction of either the gum or the resinoid with alcohol. Inferior material i.e. ungraded olibanum is satisfactory in this process.

The essential oils are purchased by manufacturers of finished perfumery products, while resinoids are used in soaps and detergents; among the users are the multinationals such as Unilever and Proctor & Gamble.

Demand for these gums is generally stable with variations between the different types. However, consumption is relatively small and therefore a crucial decision by one of the chief manufacturers regarding whether to use or exclude certain gum ingredients in a certain formulation could have a disproportionate effect on the overall consumption.

Synthetic perfumery ingredients stand as a major competitor for the derivatives of the natural gums. They have the advantage of both being cheaper and possessing persistent, predictable olfactory and chemical properties. Moreover, they are immune to supply and quality problems that face natural products. Natural ingredients will probably continue to be used despite the competition as certain elements are difficult to reproduce exactly by synthetic substitutes. Moreover, price is not considered as a major determinant of demand, since manufacturers may not opt to change formulations in response to short-term price increases, although they may consider change in the case of a substantial price increase.

European dealers in Hamburg and Marseille supply most of the ingredient manufacturers, although two of the largest consumers, Chauvet and Robertet, tend to purchase from local sources when supplies are available. European dealers and some of the consumers would like to receive goods close to their place of origin. But dealing with the public agency in Somalia and some Somali dealers is thought risky. Commitments relating to supply are reported not to be kept, claims for faulty goods are neglected if not rejected and there are perennial problems relating to quality. This prompted an intermediary role to be assumed by the more efficient and experienced dealers in Djibouti and Aden.

China is the largest consumer of natural gum-resins, olibanum (mainly Eritrean type), myrrh and opopanax. Gums have been included in China's imports since antiquity, and are used in the traditional pharmaceutical industry. Traditional medicine is still said to be popular in China, which is exploring a limited export market.

Before the 1970s when the price of *meydi* incense saw a tremendous increase due to expanded demand in the Arabian market, the Somali gum industry was of little significance to the national economy. Henrikson (1968) claimed that the revenue from natural gum exports never exceeded 1% of the total export trade value until 1960. The *meydi* incense is typically a prestige product and its demand seems to depend upon the health of the Saudi oil economy. Some of the other gums face competition from synthetic products. These facts portend future uncertainty for the natural gum industry. However, if the frankincense trade was important for the history and culture of the Somali nation in the past, today as the third largest export product, the sector has become vital for the economy of the whole country.

CHAPTER TWO

Social and property categories in Somalia

Social organisation of the Somali

The importance of lineage in the sphere of commerce was mentioned in the first chapter. Moreover, in order to understand the system of frankincense production we have to look into the organisation and functioning of the pervasive patrilineal descent system of the Somali. Through examination of property classification the overwhelming influence of pastoral ideology on local sedentary economies of frankincense and crop production in northern Somalia is made understandable.

I. M. Lewis' study of Pastoralism and politics among northern Somali (1961b)[1], offers a penetrating account of the social organisation of the Somali society. Somalis have an all-pervasive and elaborate national genealogical chart which unites the total Somali population at the highest level. The total Somali population is divided into six major clan-families—the Dir, Isaaq, Hawiye, Daarood, Digil and Raxanweyn (See Figure 1). The first four clan-families are predominantly pastoral, practising herding of camels, sheep, goats and cattle, in the semi-arid lands of the Horn. At present, these clans are widely distributed throughout the country. Their culture is quite uniform, and the minor cultural variations, as they occur, can be attribute to contact with other groups. The remaining two clan-families are mainly settled in the wetter riverain region in southern Somalia. They are characterised as chiefly agrarian groups, but practice a relatively diversified economy of agro-pastoralism.

The distinction between the dominant pastoral clan-families and cultivating southern groups is further configured in the national genealogy. The former trace descent from a common ancestor, Samaale, while the latter are descended from Sab.

There is a remarkable cultural and organisational difference between the chiefly agrarian southern groups and the pastoral clans. In the south, cultivating groups are "land-holding corporations" living in stable territories, and often composed of amalgamated groups of different ethnic origins at various stages of assimilation. They have formal offices and a more or less stratified authority structure. These features are to a great extent absent in the case of northern pastoralists and their counterparts in the south. Local contiguity is not a significant principle of social cohesion and solidarity, and agnation provides the basis of corporate interest.

---

[1] The information on the social organisation is primarily based on Lewis.

Figure 1. *The genealogical chart of the Somali*
(Source: Lewis 1961b:12)

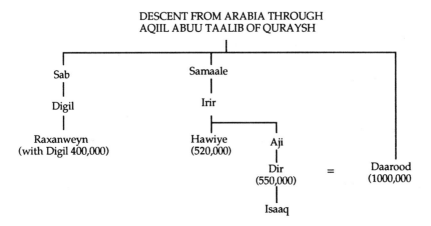

DESCENT FROM ARABIA THROUGH
AQIIL ABUU TAALIB OF QURAYSH

Sab

Digil

Raxanweyn
(with Digil 400,000)

Samaale

Irir

Hawiye
(520,000)

Aji

Dir
(550,000)   =   Daarood
(1000,000

Isaaq

Somalis are devout Sunni Muslims who follow almost exclusively the Shaafi'ite School of Law, and not surprisingly trace descent, above the clan-family, to the founders of the Arabian Islam.

Some of the larger clan-families number over a million souls, with a geneological span of no less than thirty named generations. Widely scattered geographically, this upper level of grouping is a symbolic rather than corporate political entity. Identification and loose cohesion is maintained through the common genealogical affiliation. Elders of the clan-family avidly preserve the history of the clan-family and its relations with others.

The clan-family is further segmented into different units, the largest and socially most important of which is the clan. This grouping generally marks the upper limit of corporate political action and has some territorial ties. Some of the larger clans and sub-clans have clan heads with rather nominal authority. Some clans claim more than twenty generations back to their founding ancestor.

Within the clan, the socially most important patrilineage is the "primary lineage" (of Lewis 1961b:5). To the founding ancestor, a member may count between six to ten generations. The exogamy rule and the inclination of its members to identify themselves with this group can be designated as its chief characteristics.

At the bottom of this elaborately segmented system, where every Somali is a member of a large array of patrilineages, lies the *dia*-paying group—corporate members tied together by collective responsibility to pay and receive blood compensation or *dia*. This significant social unit can be seen as the basic jural and political unit of Somali society. It is a small lineage or an alliance of small lineages, with a strength of between a few hundred to a few thousand members, and with a genealogical span of between four to eight generations. (See Figure 2.)

The *dia*-paying unit guarantees a pastoral Somali security of life and property, security against raid and feud, pastoral scourges that were rampant in the past. It is also the social unit which regulates an individual's access to the natural resources. Mobilising the existing strong ties of agnation and the binding contract which is emphasised at this level of grouping, law and order is most markedly maintained by elders in this patrilineage. Traditional group leaders, *Akils*, had been institutionalised by past governments, both colonial and independent civilian governments, in rather elusive attempts to introduce instituted authority in the nomadic world.

Somalis are organised on the principle of patrilineal descent. The all-pervasive national genealogy, whose major points of cleavage are noted above, allows men to trace descent through the maleline to a common ancestor. Thus kinship establishes a man's politico-jural position in the community and his relations with others. To express the Somali political philosophy and its fundamental function, Lewis cited a much-quoted local axiom: "What a person's address is in Europe, his genealogy is in Somaliland. By virtue of his genealogy of birth, each individual has an exact place in society and within a very wide range of agnatic kinship it is possible for each person to trace his precise connection with everyone else. Somali political philosophy is thus an evaluation of agnatic connection" (Lewis 1961b:2).

Figure 2. *Morphology of the segmentary lineage system of the Somali*
(Source: Lewis 1961b:4)

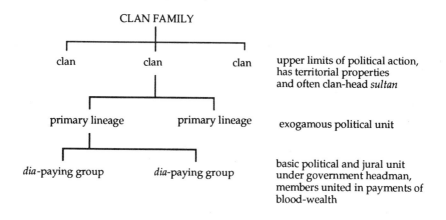

Without undermining the principle of agnation, *tol*, as the basis of corporate function in Somali society, a supplementary principle of contract, *xeer*, is utilised as an expedient cultural element that defines politico-jural cohesion.

To redress the balance where there is disparity between the actual strength of the opposing patrilineages in competition for scarce and seasonally varying pastoral resources, Somalis utilise contractual alliance within the framework of the lineage system. They do not manipulate genealogy or resort to putative kinship to attain the desired relationship between social units. Existing matrilateral ties, but sometimes also putative uterine kinship, are also employed for the same purpose—to redress the imbalance between the social units on the ground. Local contiguity is not the fundamental principle of cohesion and collaboration. There are no stable territorial groups, and ties to a fixed territory are to a great extent lacking. This affords the principle of agnation a functional primacy.

Most of the larger interior trading towns in northern Somalia are of recent formation and there is a striking cultural continuity between urban towns and rural areas. The tendency to replicate lineage affiliation with area of residence in an urban setting is very strong. This is more marked in smaller villages where town planning has little affected this pattern.

Elders permanently or temporarily residing in towns and often possessing urban property direct lineage affairs. Moreover, traders and other kinsmen living in towns are subject to the *dia*-paying contract of their rural clansmen.

Economic cooperation between close kinsmen living in the two domains is as binding as politico-jural links. Most of the largely transitional generation townsmen own rural property of pastoral herds, agricultural or frankincense fields, in the country of their lineage. Such property which was acquired before migration as potential members of their groups, is managed and exploited by rural kinsmen.

Some traders and employed townsmen sponsor the education of a child or children of their nomadic brothers and other close agnates, or younger brothers and sisters from a second marriage of their nomadic father. Those who can afford it usually finance the construction of water tanks for the pastoral family of close agnates. In their competition to obtain the assistance and admiration of a rich kinsman living in the town, rural agnates sometimes wildly accuse each other of damaging the corporate interest of the composite families in the rural area.

Visiting kinsmen from the country usually bring gifts of pastoral delicacies, like purified ghee and small pieces of dried meat cooked with the animal fat to urbanised close agnates. Sometimes a ram is brought to urban families to be slaughtered for a special occasion, or to satisfy the desire for meat. Also if someone in the village desires a change, or feels feeble, he may go to the nomadic hamlet of his close agnate during the rainy season of plenty, to regale with the fresh milk of the camel which is thought to have the power to recuperate the weak.

Assistance from nomadic kinsmen is essential for poor urban agnates, who may require the proceeds from an obtained animal for a particular purpose, such as the fee for a driving licence. But the gifts offered to rich kinsmen in the towns are symbolic rather than necessary. Nomadic kinsmen usually receive in return an amount of cash or consumer products and food whose total cost may exceed the value of their gift. Indeed, on many occasions, pastoral gifts are assumed as a pretext to visit a wealthy kinsman in the town to seek assistance.

Pastoral and non-pastoral categories of property

In Somali, the generic term for wealth is *maal* (alternative *adduunyo*, worldly material things, or *xoolo* which refers to "animate" wealth). *Maal* is also commonly used to refer to the surplus animals or agricultural fields that are loaned to needy kinsmen. The compound term *soo maal* which means "go and milk" the livestock, is a popular version for the origin of the word Somali (cf. Lewis 1961b:12). These designations of the word *maal* express the pastoral outlook of the society.

The schematic representation of wealth is not complex, for only two distinct and non-overlapping broad categories are generally acknowledged. The first is the pastoral type of wealth, and consists exclusively of nomadic livestock species and other domestic animals that render some sort of service to the pastoral people. The second category groups together all other useful properties that fall outside the first category.

The linguistic regional terms that correspond to the major categories of wealth are socially important. Regional differences with respect to the description of wealth, accord with the social division of the Somali society into two factions: the predominantly pastoral groups in northern Somalia and the largely sedentary cultivating groups in southern Somalia.

In the northern part of the country, the terms *mood* and *nool* are most commonly used to express categories of wealth. *Nool* literally means "living", but more appropriately it can be translated as "animate wealth" or more precisely as pastoral property. The *mood* concept literally designates something non-living or dead, but it accurately seems to correspond to "inanimate" or "non-pastoral" form of property. In the chiefly sedentary groups in the south, property concepts that correspond to those in the north are *guure* and *maguure* which mean literally: "mobile" and "immobile".

Fundamentally the two regional systems of property classification are identical. Not only two broad categories of wealth are commonly acknowledged, but also the elements that are placed under each category are similar. The "animate" or "pastoral" northern concept and its southern counterpart "mobile", consists of the familiar domestic stock of pastoral people, while the "inanimate" or "non-pastoral" and "immobile" category represents wealth other than the nomadic stock.

If the two regional property classification systems are basically identical in terms of differentiating pastoral and non-pastoral forms of wealth, their descriptions vary to designate the distinct variation of the two factions of Somali society. To glorify cherished herds, northern pastoralists describe nomadic herds as *nool* which imply "living" in the literal sense, in contrast to non-pastoral property which is designated as *mood* or "non-living" and by implication inferior, undesired wealth. For their part, sedentary communities in the south exalt the primary resource of land which is described as "immobile" landed property *maguure*, a notion which seems to convey a sense of permanency in contrast to the "mobile" *guure* pastoral herds which depend upon varying and uncertain pastoral resources.

The "animate or pastoral" category of wealth is self-explanatory. It encompasses herds of camels, flocks of sheep and goats, horses, donkeys and mules whose service, to varying degrees, is required for animal husbandry. In short, this form of wealth represents the herding species that support the pastoral clans. Of these, the camel, which has been described by I. M. Lewis (*ibid*.:86) as the "capital resource" of the Somali pastoralists, is the most coveted form of wealth.

The "inanimate or non-pastoral" category is polarised as distinct from the pastoral type of property. The first thing to note about this ill-defined category is that it does not have the distinctiveness afforded to the other. It is a set of various property elements explained or categorised in terms of what it is not, rather than what it actually is (it is not animate or pastoral property). Hence it is a residual category of wealth, for any valuable asset other than the domestic herds are indiscriminately assembled under this extraneous jumble of property elements that are seen as alien to the pastoral society.

The importance of inanimate wealth is that it can accommodate any novel property which may evolve as a result of chance. The lack of definition induces elasticity to the system of classification and allows a flexibility that insulates it from disruption or endemic contradiction. Any useful material object that is not "animate" can conveniently be counted as non-pastoral, regardless of any of its other important characteristics.

Property elements jumbled together under the residual and open "inanimate" category include useful items such as money, jewellery and gold, capital goods, land and agricultural products, wild plant products, weaponry, trucks, building property, enterprise etc.

To propose a simple model for the property classification outlined in the above, the two categories of wealth may not be regarded as two distinct and separately bounded sets. A suitable schematic representation would be a framework consisting of a central circle which encloses an exclusively pastoral property. All other types of "inanimate" wealth occur outside the central circle which encloses the "animate wealth".

Figure 3. *General classification of property*

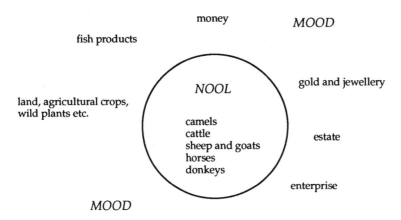

What needs to be stressed is the fact that the classification alluded to in the above is constructed from the actor's perspective, particularly from the pastoralist's outlook. Nevertheless, the distinction between pastoral and non-pastoral wealth is also used by the other economic groups in northern Somalia, frankincense collectors in the northeast, and sedentary cultivators in the northwest.

To substantiate the significance of the actor's categorisation of property, northern pastoralists do not count poultry as animal property. Rearing chicken is alien to mobile nomads and does not constitute a source of food. As a result of this, poultry is seen as "birds" which are not hunted or valued for other significant reasons.

Pastoral concepts used to categorise property are apparently different from the specialised wealth concepts used in the developed world. To clarify the categories I will therefore give some examples of actual situations where these indigenous ideas are put use. Important social transactions between groups are customarily settled in terms of quantified "animate" and "inanimate" units, depending upon the size of the transaction concerned. For instance, in the case of sustained physical injury by a man of a particular lineage, the elders of the lineage of the victim would negotiate with those of the assailant's lineage, to come to a peaceful settlement of the matter. Quite often, the final negotiated compensation would consist of a sum total expressed in "animate" and "inanimate" units.

The bridewealth (people in the frankincense region know it as honouring affines, *xurmo*) which is exchanged between the groom's social unit and the bride's lineage, may be settled with a payment consisting of both units of wealth; for example, 15 camels *nool* and a certain amount of cash or a gun, *mood* (cf. Lewis *ibid.*:138–139).

To account for the rationale of the indigenous property classification is not as easy as the overall distinction made between "animate" and "inanimate" categories. The first clue for the basis of the classification can be traced in the structure of the scheme, in other words the polarisation between "pastoral" and "non-pastoral" forms of property. The coveted pastoral herd units that are described as "living" in the literal sense, are separated from the "inanimate" wealth described as "non-living" and by implication inferior to herds.

Camels and small stock

Varying attitudes apply to the different species raised by nomads, although pastoral wealth in general is held to be superior to non-pastoral property. The division is fundamentally based on ecological requirements accompanied by a distinction in the values which attach to the two types of stock. Sheep and goats have importance mainly in subsistence while camels have a greater social value since in addition to their subsistence uses they are regarded primarily as a medium for the regulation of most aspects of social, and political life. (Lewis 1961b:88–89).

The influence of camel culture on the world view of the pastoral and non-pastoral economic groups in the northern region will become clear in chapter six which explores the oral poetry of the frankincense sector. In general, the fate of the Somalis is thought to be inextricably linked to the existence of the camel herds. It is very difficult for a pastoralist to contemplate life without camels. The ideological association between camels and the continuity of the lineage is symbolised by the image of camel herds. Apart from joint interests and corporate joint rights over the total camel stock of the lineage, the camel stock of individual members of the lineage usually bear lineage brands; in contrast, herds of small stock bear the brand of the individual owner.

Idealised as the "capital resource" of the pastoral society, and symbolised as a corporate property which is expressed in joint watering of the camel stock of the group and joint protection, it is not surprising to observe strong "ownership" rights at the individual level. The generosity attributed to pastoral Somalis hardly applies when it comes to camels. Needy kin are preferably offered some sheep or goats but rarely camels. Yet a destitute close kinsman, a brother or an uncle, may be given a valuable burden camel or a female milk camel. If a rich pastoralist feels it essential to assist a beloved kinsman, he will lend camel *maal* rather than give them outright.

Coveted camels pass between social groups ceremonially on important social occasions. The example of homicide compensation, most clearly shows the reluctance shown by individual herders to give away camels. Individual members of the lineage which is paying compensation collectively to the victim's lineage, will strive to pay with the least desired camels in their herd at the time. The consequence of this tendency is that the final compensation paid for homicide consists usually of an inferior herd. It is proverbial among northern pastoralists to wonder about inferior camels, if they are camels selected for the payment of blood money—*ma geel magbaa!*

If the desire to keep camels and hoard them sometimes transcends kinship morality, it is no less the case that it also violates a religious prescription. Except for the pious, most camel herders exempt their camel stock from the Islamic annual obligatory tax *saka* on property. The tendency of those who pay is to offer inferior camels.

The desire to acquire camels is best articulated by a famous northern poet, Abdi Gaheyr. In response to a religious man who suggested that pastoralists must cease plundering the herds of fellow Muslims, Abdi Gaheyr places camel affairs above the rule of Islam. Here are the relevant lines from his poem:

> Other clans send their children as migrant labour to Aden
> Among the Iidagale clan someone without camels is not counted
> among the ranks in the group. (4)

Other clans with substantial numbers of townsmen are said to be able to send adult men to Aden in southern Yemen which was an important labour market before independence in 1960. These relatively urbanised clans which could earn remittances are distinguished from the poet's interior clan which is predominantly pastoral. Without camels, the fate of the members of the pastoral Iidagale clan is described to be uncertain or rather in limbo as the second line seems to suggest.

In a highly secular tone uncharacteristic of devout Somalis, in another more familiar poem, the poet finds a place for the camel in the afterlife, notwithstanding its indispensable role in this world. Here is a relevant extract:

> The progenitor female camel *Idinba'as*, its burden camel and young calves
> Have benefitted the early companions and revered supporters of Prophet Muhammad
> Someone without camels is said to earn no praise in the afterlife
> Why should a person without camels pray with you, men of religion. (5)

In terms of Islamic ideology, forgiveness, penitence and expiation, with which the devout may earn heaven, must be the overriding concerns. Such subjects as camels that indeed come after people in importance in this world are not important in the other. To the displeasure of the pious, if the secular poet transgressed the border of the devout by extending the importance of the camel to the afterlife, he surely emphasised the immense love Somalis have for the camel.

The importance of the camel is ceremonially enacted at the birth of a baby boy by the husband who is the proprietor of the family stock. The infant is offered a gift of a female camel known as *xuddun-xidh* or "naval knot", the nucleus of the future herd of the newborn son. And as the child grows he receives gifts of camels from his father, and sometimes from his uncle and other members of the male kin. As shown in chapter three on ownership, women do not inherit camels; these are passed from father to son.

Sometimes a husband may give a female camel to console an offended wife whose dignity he has damaged. If it reproduces , the husband may withdraw the offer and dispossess the wife. If the wife complains to her husband's kinsmen, whose support a good wife obtains for good reason, or else to kinsmen in her natal group, she may be told to forget claiming camels. Camels belong to men, not women.

Idealised as the "capital" goods of pastoral peoples, and as a lineage resource, not to mention its social and symbolic value, it is understandable that the camel occupies a pivotal position in the culture of Somali society. Although they cherish it highly, Somalis do not consider the camel as sacred in the literal sense. To assert its uniqueness in relation to the small stock and non-pastoral property, pastoralists find it difficult to describe its attraction, and call it a property of the "anthropomorphic spirits", *xoolo jin*. It is not an ordinary property, the protection or acquisition of which a man can sacrifice his life for. The camel has been a constant cause of pastoral feuds and vendettas in the past and is still the source of many conflicts.

Sheep and goats are often sold to be exchanged for supplementary food items and other household goods. In contrast, camels are rarely brought to the market. If this happens, as it may at times, it is usually impelled by sheer necessity. Usually camels sold and taken from the *kraal* are inferior individual camels; for instance, an old female camel no longer reproducing, or one that is deficient and not becoming pregnant, or yet another with diseased udders. Somalis know this tendency and do not buy female camels which they want to rear directly from the market; instead they buy directly from the owner of a camel whose pedigree they know.

The proceeds from surplus male camels may partly be invested in a female calf that will increase the herd in the future and partly finance other needs. Sometimes a pastoralist sells some sheep and goats and exchanges part of the proceeds for a female camel to build up the camel herd at the expense of the other less valuable species.

In contrast to camel herds which are viewed as "permanent pastoral wealth" and lineage property, small stock of sheep and goats are seen as consumer domestic goods. Northern pastoralists say *geel waa raasamaal arina waa raashin* , "camels are permanent wealth while sheep and goats are food". The concept of the camel as permanent pastoral wealth is indeed engendered by its profound social and symbolic values in addition to its subsistence utility.

Camels are status symbols, "beget" women, and maintain relations between groups. Camels paid to the lineage of a murdered man by that of the assailant are said not to compensate entirely the value of the dead man (Somalis do not put a value on a person as the classical literature tends to suggest) but to make relatives forget the tragic human loss. Even in terms of subsistence, camels are supreme. They are drought animals and withstand the arid conditions in the Horn more than the other stock. They are economical on water which is a scarce commodity, and can move fast and frequently across the country to make the best use of the available resources. These qualities of the camel, not matched by the small stock and cattle, further entrench the notion of the camel as permanent wealth and reliable stock in adversity.

The designation of the small stock as consumer domestic goods in contrast to the more permanent and lineage camel herds, is also demonstrated by the difference in the management of the two pastoral stocks. Sheep and goats are commonly herded by household female labour in the nomadic hamlet, while boys and unmarried adult men tend camels in the camel-camp. Of all the pastoral wealth, the Somali pony was most valuable in the past. This was largely because of its essential role in the protection of the lives and property of pastoral people in a world endemic with conflict.

It is interesting to note that the love Somalis hold for livestock seems to be extended to animal products. The traditional pastoral diet of milk and meat, now supplemented with imported or locally-produced food stuff, is thought to be the best and most nourishing food. Pastoral Somalis are often said to manifest certain qualities that help them weather the harsh nomadic lifestyle: resilience, virility, unyielding resistance to thirst and hunger etc. These qualities are thought by pastoralists to be obtained from the consumption of livestock products.

A pastoralist would taunt a visiting kinsman from the town as being effeminate, someone who cannot adequately perform the usual laborious pastoral chores, driving camels to distant wells in the dry season. In towns, he may argue, people do simple clerical work even the weak women folk could perform. A pastoral stereotype holds that the hands of townsmen are clean and tender, not hardened by rough manual work, that an ordinary sheet of paper can cut through like a sharp knife. The physical weakness pastoralists assume to be characteristic of townspeople is explained as a consequence of the latter's diet, which contains little pastoral products, and largely consists of inferior items like vegetables, fruit, fish, rice, spaghetti etc.

The positive attitude toward animal products is further enhanced by the medicinal virtues the pastoral diet is thought to possess. The first traditional treatment for a sick person, before anything else, is to treat him with a dose of specially prepared meat or milk or purified *ghee* sometimes taken with non-pastoral food. This tendency prevails in rural areas and depends upon strong beliefs about the medicinal attributes of pastoral products. It is sometimes carried out without consideration for the types of illnesses that are anathema to the consumption of dairy products, such as jaundice. People who urgently require special care, for example a circumcised child, a delivered mother, an injured person a weak person, are given specially prepared meat, milk and purified *ghee*.

Apparently the pastoralist model of property classification is biased against non-pastoral forms of wealth. Unlike the pastoral stocks where different values are attached to different stocks, non-pastoral property is not systematically categorised and there are no coherent values attached to different elements. The pastoral attitude towards these types of property is distinctly negative— inferior and devoid of the social and symbolic value pastoral herds perform. Non-pastoral agricultural crops are said to be inferior because they are not as nourishing as pastoral products. For a pastoralist, those who till the land are poor in spirit and in livestock, for cattle and ploughing oxen replace camel to a considerable extent (Lewis 1961b:100–101).

The pastoralist view of fishing and fish products is even more lowly and degrading than that obtaining for agricultural crops. While pastoralists consume substantial quantities of grains produced by rival cultivators, particularly in the dry season, they do not eat fish, and hence their denigration of fish is most pronounced. "Fish eater" is a term of abuse. Eating fish is repugnant and one informant asserted that the sight of raw fish or talk about it makes him feel nauseated. A pastoralist may describe fishing as "maritime hunting" to reduce it to a form of hunting, for he derides hunting. The pastoralist dislike for fish can even be observed in larger towns in the north where the fish market is relatively small compared to that of livestock meat.

A pastoral saying meditates upon the fate of an unwise man who sold his pack camel: *Allahayow maxey noqon ninkii awrkii lacaq siistey!*—"I wonder what would happen to a man who exchanged his burden camel which is essential for herding, for cash". This old saying indicates that livestock, particularly camels, are preferred to cash, a tendency which may still be true despite current thorough commercialisation of the national herd. Urban property such as buildings and cash are thought less permanent and artificial. They may disappear as quickly as they are acquired and are therefore unreliable, unlike the camel herd which always supports nomads even in adversity.

The social and property value of frankincense trees

Frankincense-gathering communities and sedentary cultivators in the northwest region of Somalia do not contradict the pastoral property classification distinguishing "pastoral" and "non-pastoral" categories of wealth. However, they praise or glorify their respective economic basis in the same spirit pastoralists praise coveted herds. In chapter six the competition for honour and excellence between economic groups in the northern part of Somalia via the media of the poetic oral craft will be discussed. We will see how the dominant camel culture influences the outlook of non-pastoral groups who sing of agricultural or frankincense fields being as valuable as camels. Frankincense collectors and sedentary cultivators view their primary resources with fascination. Working on the camel standard which Somalis use to evaluate important things in life, frankincense collectors point out certain advantages commercial forests excel in.

Frankincense gathering is claimed to be more viable than herding, for the reason that it is possible for herd-poor families with a very limited herd size (less than fifty head of sheep and goats) to subsist on incense production. With an insufficient number of stock, poor families cannot rely on nomadism since a large herd of more than a hundred sheep and goats and some camels is necessary for subsistence of an average pastoral family with six or seven family members.

People's fascination with their frankincense forests cannot adequately be explained by the simplistic device of giving credit to a resource that sustains the communities of incense collectors. A complete explanation must consider ideology. Muslim Somalis believe that compassionate Allah justly provided each community he created on the earth with a primary resource to subsist upon. By His will the physical environment of every social group is moulded and modelled in such a way as to sustain the basic resource for the maintenance and well-being of each and every social group, regardless of its colour, creed and ideology. In the light of this belief, incense-producing communities in the frankincense region of Somalia see frankincense property primarily as their legitimate share in Allah's equitable distribution of resources. As good Muslims, they must not complain whatever the merit and demerit of their respective resource; they must try to make the best possible use out of whatever resource they were given as a result of Allah's providence.

Apart from the ideology which enjoins Muslims to be thankful for what Allah has provided for them and be content with it, incense people like other economic groups often complain about their lot.[2] For the people in the frankincense region, the disparity of resource distribution at the national level seems to be obvious. The southern region of Somalia contains the most fertile and well-watered agricultural land. Most of the land in the northern part of the country is blessed with the best available pasturage in relation to the rugged and mountainous resource-poor frankincense region. Given the limited resource base of their country, incense people seem to embrace the view that, in a sense, they have been compensated by benign Allah in providing unique and localised commercial forests.

The divine compassion of Allah towards the frankincense-cultivating communities is revealed in a miraculous story about the original formation of the frankincense groves told by informants in Bosaso district. The creation myth claims that frankincense groves in a form identical to their present nature were cruising through the sky to an unspecified destination. At the time they were aloft the frankincense region, they were very tired from the effects of the flight. Desperate to rest, they entreated the maritime incense region for an overnight lodging which was allowed. Once landed, frankincense groves declined to honour their guest status and refused to abandon the region. In this miraculous story, frankincense resource had been created for the benefit of the communities inhabiting the resource-poor territory which is not suitable for agriculture nor for pastoral production. The obstinacy of the Boswellia forests, that is their refusal to abandon incense territory, has become an admonitory expression which is applied against fastidious persons who persistently ask for support, or those who repeat irksome mistakes against somebody who is patient with them.

The assumption among incense communities that they have been kindly compensated with the frankincense resource is indicated by other factors. Incense collection areas, *xiji*, are described as fields. Territorially bounded collection areas could be considered as fields in the sense that they are plots of land growing exploited commercial crops and also because of the fact that they are subject to rights.[3]

Similarities and differences between frankincense and agricultural fields in the northwest sedentary region are discussed in chapter three. Here I only want to give an example relating to a tendency in which incense collectors describe their chief resource as "camels" in poetic allusion—a tendency to impart the love Somalis hold for camels to incense groves, or possibly an explanatory device characteristic of the pastoral Somalis who draw on camel metaphors in order to explain non-pastoral property. This epigram which was obtained from Galgala village in Bosaso district exalts commercial frankincense forests to the rank of camels.

In the verse, frankincense forests are figuratively spoken of as camels. In the first line the resin derived from incense plants is likened to the milk obtained from female camels. The second line implies that just as the good female camel

---

[2] This will be evident in chapter six.
[3] See chapter three on ownership.

will yield a full *gaawa* milk vessel, so a fecund frankincense tree produces a full collecting basket of commercial resin. Frankincense collectors carry the dichotomy further by calling a fecund frankincense tree, *meydi*, which is a popular name for a female camel that yields plenty of milk. Conversely, an incense plant that produces less resin is known as *biqjaar* which is also a name for a camel that produces less milk.

> We have got camels (frankincense forests) that never run dry of milk (resin)
> Each individual camel yields a full milk vessel *gaawa*
> Camels whose lips do not have to be brought to the water
> Camels that are never troubled by hunger
> Camels that grow in the frankincense Guban region. (6)

In the third and fourth lines, the poet remarks on some qualities in which frankincense forests excel the coveted camels. They are resistant to hunger which may decimate the sturdy camel herds in a prolonged drought; and they thrive on minimal rainfall of four inches per annum, and are therefore more economical on water which is scarce in the Horn. The final line is a clue for the reader, to help him understand the type of camels concerned. The expression "camels that grow in the frankincense Guban region" is a sufficient indication for a Somali to recognise that the topic of discussion is not actual camels, but frankincense forests that are as valuable or more important than the cherished camels which do not thrive in the burnt coastal Guban (incense) region.

The specific attitude of the inhabitants of the frankincense region towards incense property is one replete with fascination and marvel. It is not easy to say if this is entirely due to innocuous eccentric glorification of the primary resource, or a defence against the domineering pastoral culture. I surmise it is both.

Various reasons seem to account for the uniqueness attributed to the Boswellia forests. First and foremost is perhaps their natural habitat. They grow, particularly the <u>Boswellia frereana</u> species, outwards and upwards from vertical cliffs, clinging on the surface of boulders by means of "a bulbous mass". There is much debate among the frankincense collectors as to whether frankincense trees growing on exposed rock surfaces are held to their sites by natural roots, the "bulbous mass" or some other mysterious force. This feature of the plants has also attracted the fascination of various observers who frequently mention it in their reports (e.g. Miles 1872:64).

To argue against domestication experiments going on in the frankincense region and outside it, some collectors and inhabitants in the region tend to argue that to plant precious forests on extremely precarious sites must surely be the work of an omnipotent and divine power, that of Allah. The creation of wonderful things, such as frankincense species, is thought to be tangible evidence that the Almighty exposes himself to human society, for the purpose of strengthening their belief. The creation of all wonderful things is accepted as the domain of Allah. This notion may be exemplified by the public perception which disregards the possibility of propagating frankincense trees. The establishment of recent experimental state domestication farms is seen by many as the pursuit of the impossible and meddling in the sphere of the omnipotent. The human power to create things is limited, and propagation of exotic incense species is thought a futile exercise by reckless humans attempting to transcend the limits of their power.

Apart from the habitat of the fabulous incense trees, people derive great delight and pride from the long-standing export history of the incense crop. The cumulative effect of these factors have generated an impressive attitude towards frankincense property. However, there are no mystical attitudes attached to them, despite the traditional use of incense. They are marvelled at in moments of speculation, highly regarded in public discourse concerning objects of importance, and above all are economically exploited without any stringent ritual observance. This noted pragmatism is fairly true of northern Somalis in general. As mentioned in the above, Somalis do not consider their beloved camel herds as sacred, nor do sedentary cultivators in Borama district relate mystical forces to their agricultural land.

Non-pastoral groups in northern Somalia boast of essential resources of frankincense and agricultural land. These resources are assumed by the respective sedentary groups as lineage resources, the same way camels are exalted as lineage wealth by nomads.[4] Women do not inherit these group properties, which are passed from father to son and by implication through men of the patriline.

What may be said to differentiate pastoral wealth from non-pastoral property of frankincense and agricultural lands is that the latter do not generally pass between social units and between members of the lineage. Camels, though coveted, are passed between social units ceremonially on important occasions such as the exchange system involving blood compensation. More commonly the smaller stock take part in frequent social prestations. Apart from right of use in relation to sedentary resources, do not circulate the same way stock circulate between individual members of a lineage and between different social units, as pastoral livestock do. This role is performed by the crops procured from the sedentary property of fixed land. Sedentary resources of frankincense and agricultural land are fixed and immobile. They may be affixed to social relations among kinsmen or affines through right of use, but usually are not passed between "owners" and non-holders.

The dependence of non-pastoral groups on nomadic culture for images and metaphors, seems to reduce them to localised systems struggling to attain independent identity within the constraint of an overarching pastoral tradition.[5] The pastoral supremacy in the Somali culture and its influence on sedentary systems is understandable because of the recent introduction of agriculture in the northwest, at the beginning of the twentieth century, and the fact that pastoralism is a subordinate activity to the prevailing peasant economies of frankincense and crop production. Moreover, the substantial influence of nomadic culture on the frankincense economy, which is as old as pastoralism if not older, signifies the tenacity of pastoralism in Somali culture.

The pastoral model of property classification which is applied throughout the country testifies to the intensity of the influence of nomadic values upon the Somalis. Values evolved by pastoral wealth are relatively universal. Since both social and symbolic values revolve around this property, it is regarded as a superior form of wealth. Table 1 summarises the chief characteristics of major property types discussed in the text.

---

[4] Group ideologies, inheritance patterns and other characteristics of group resources among northern economic groups are dealt with in chapter three.

[5] See chapter six on poetry.

The pastoral attitude towards urban properties such as money, buildings etc. is ambiguous. Although these may be coveted, they are rated as being less reliable and less important than rural property of herds or land and frankincense forests. Because of the cultural commitment of pastoralists towards their stock, and the hold pastoralism has had over non-pastoral communities, there is apparently a general tendency to reduce other types of wealth to pastoral or "animate" property. In both rural and urban areas, it is usually the case that blood compensation is conveniently valued in terms of camels. Since it is not practical to effect the compensation in actual camels between lineages, a sum calculated on contractual camel price which is much lower than the real market value of the camel is paid.

Table 1. *Chief characteristics of the "animate" and "inanimate" categories of wealth*

"ANIMATE" OR PASTORAL WEALTH (CAMELS, SHEEP, GOATS)	"INANIMATE" OR NON-PASTORAL WEALTH (FRANKINCENSE FORESTS, AGRICULTURAL LAND)
socially and physically mobile	fixed and socially not as mobile as the other
invigorating animal products	less nourishing plant food
universal system of values	local system of values
frequently constitute part of the social exchange	do not often pass between lineages

CHAPTER THREE

Ownership and utilisation of the frankincense fields

Pastoral and agricultural landuse systems

Since the frankincense tenurial arrangement embodies some of the chief features of the sedentary and pastoral landuse economies, it will be useful to outline briefly the major forms of landuse systems in the country. Compared to other African nations very few intensive local studies have been undertaken in Somalia. More surprisingly, the most important studies on land tenure, however inadequate, were carried out in the colonial period. Neither the Siyaad Barre government, perhaps due to its cooperativisation experiment and the underlying collective exploitation of land resources, nor the preceding civilian governments did anything remarkable to augment the meagre colonial literature on the subject.

For the time of the Siyaad Barre regime, seeking information about local landuse systems creates problems for research students. It is illegal to discuss the clan organisation on which these systems are actually based. Furthermore, information about the processes of land registration, however unreliable and inadequate, is sensitive, as is arbitration, since they involve the interests of influential urban settlers and powerful interest groups with vested interests in land. Rich and powerful urban settlers moving out into rural areas, particularly in the potentially rich agricultural lands in the southern region, constitute a current tendency that is widely acknowledged but not yet well researched.

The land tenure system in Somalia is fundamentally based on the pervasive principle of clan organisation. Customary norms which relate to the social organisation ultimately regulate individual and group access to the important material things that are locally available.

As we have seen, an elaborately segmented patrilineal descent system ultimately divides the total Somali population into six large "clan families". Each clan family subdivides into different social units, the largest and most important of which is the clan. Unlike the clan family which indeed is a higher order symbolic grouping that is too large to act as a single unit, the clan acts as a political entity when the combined strength of the clan is required to achieve a common end. For the present purpose, the clan is important for it represents a social corporation that is associated with a particular territory. Within the clan, the socially most important unit is the primary lineage. At the bottom of the social organisation lies the "*dia*-paying group". (See previous chapter).

Pasturage and water are the two most important elements which are essential for pastoral production. Surface grazing and browse are primarily regulated by the customary principle which sanctions their unlimited access. A similar rule applies to naturally-occurring surface water.

Given the scarcity and uneven distribution of water and range in the arid northern region of Somalia, the principle of free access to seasonally and annually varying nomadic resources, can appropriately be considered as a cultural element which promotes their widest possible use. This tendency to exclude encumbrances from the utilisation of such resources is further reinforced by a strongly held Islamic tradition which demands that such properties be used publicly.

The following quotations illustrate the Islamic provisions that regulate the free disposal of water in relation to human and animal consumption: "There are three persons whom Allah will ignore on the day of the resurrection. He will not grant them any indulgence and will inflict on them painful punishment; these persons are: the man who, having enough water in excess of his herds, refuses it to a traveller..." And for animals: "...he who digs a well in the desert when there is pasture nearby cannot prevent the animals from slaking their thirst at the well." (Caponera 1954:15–16).

In contrast to naturally-occurring water which is a communal resource, two types of man-made water points are subject to prescribed rights. These are the traditional lineage wells and the increasingly common cement-lined water tanks *barkads* and artificial ponds, *ballis*.

Barkads and *ballis* mainly contain water after the poorly maintained and often shallow community points dry up during the dry season. In some areas man-made water points which are resorted to after the drying of community holes also fail to provide sufficient water for the community, particularly if rain fell later than expected. This makes long treks to the most reliable traditional wells necessary in the case of a prolonged dry season.

Man-made *barkads* and *ballis* are the property of the extended family rather than the lineage. They belong to those who invest in their construction. Their chief purpose is to secure the water demand of the owning family and its stock, in essence to protect the family and its property from the consequence of cyclical drought. In many cases, a subsidiary commercial incentive is an underlying motive. Surplus water is sold to the inhabitants of rural areas who do not own such relatively expensive facilities and therefore have to pay for the use of water at the private holes. The consequence with respect to the private holes is that the owning families, especially in the pastoral economy, are well placed in relation to the non-owning majority to exploit effectively the traditional public property.

Constructing and maintaining wells is a collective enterprise. An able-bodied man who refuses to participate in the task has traditionally been subjected to corporal punishment known as *yake* among the Gadabuursi clan in the northwest. The reluctant man was tied to the trunk of a big tree inhabited by ants. Ant bites cause pain and suffering. Furthermore, one of his precious animals was slaughtered for the labouring kinsmen. This was compensation for the labour withdrawal. Hence the disciplined kinsman was not denied the use of the well after it was completed.

The domestic and livestock water requirement of the owning lineage is paramount. Nevertheless, if the supply of the source exceeds the demand, the surplus is customarily allowed to be used by members of other social units who may need it. In contrast to the customary free access to naturally-occurring water, and the usually contractual distribution of water contained in the lineage wells, water use in man-made holes operates on commercial principles.

Government-run motorised *ballis* and *barkads*, with varying regional distribution and often serving settled communities, are generally limited. Where they occur in rural areas people are charged nominal fees.

In the pastoral world, clans may not in practice always occupy a particular region in a given season and from one year to another. However, frequent exploitation, effective occupation, implicit state tolerance of the status quo, and the existence of the traditional wells and trading villages, all constitute important factors that establish customary association between a clan and a particular territory among the northern Somalis.

The organisational differences between the dominant pastoral Somalis in the north and the chiefly agrarian groups in southern Somalia has been well documented by Lewis (i.e. 1961b, 1969b). He argued that use rights in agricultural land are individually held in the south, and the clans that maintain these rights are large, relatively more stable, territorially bounded, and moreover, to a certain degree hierarchical and stratified, with a kind of differentiated authority structure not found in the egalitarian pastoral lifestyle of the north (Lewis 1969b:59–78). These large agricultural units act as *dia*-paying groups.

Apart from individual rights held over agricultural fields and a developing concept of loyalty to a fixed territory, recently sedentarised northwestern cultivators generally lack some of the more complex institutional features of their agricultural counterparts in the south of Somalia. In the south a non-kin member could be adopted by the land-holding social unit. He is given rights and duties which are similar to those enjoyed by members of the host group (cf. *ibid.*:66). This is alien to the sedentary cultivators in the northwest, where almost all members of the sedentary village community belong to the land-holding lineage.

The sedentarisation of previously nomadic groups in the northwest which took place in the beginning of the twentieth century, has been modelled on the pastoral tenurial pattern (cf. Lewis 1961a:106–108). Each lineage settled and developed the territory customarily associated with it in the country of the clan.

In contemporary Somalia, as in some other developing countries, the crucial issue concerns the antithesis between customary norms which maintain group control over important local resources, and statutory laws that tend to deny or undermine traditional regulations. For instance, the 1975 land law declared land to be the property of the state, although in practice the mobility of pastoralists remained to a large extent unhindered, exempting land losses in some areas as a result of state regulation. Apart from concessions given to the previous land-holders, the law did not specify any rights concerning the dominant pastoral peoples in the country.

Initial distribution of frankincense trees

The frankincense system of landuse articulates important concepts that underlie both sedentary and pastoral systems of landuse. It establishes prescriptive rights over territorially-bounded frankincense collection areas locally known as incense fields. These belong to a core of closely related agnatic families. Despite being held collectively, such control rights are comparable to the individual rights held by small producers over a cultivable plot of land in the sedentary area in the northwest where sorghum is chiefly produced.

Prescriptive rights held over frankincense fields specifically relate to the most important property that occurs in the fields which are the commercially exploited frankincense species. Pasturage, naturally occurring surface water and other natural wild products which are found in the fields are communal property. By its lack of restraint on nomadic resources, the system enshrines an important pastoral principle which promotes free access to pasturage and water.

Rights to frankincense-bearing species were initially distributed according to custom as in the case of the northwestern cultivators. Lineages assumed rights over the commercial forests that grew in the areas customarily associated with them. However, all the individual members of the units concerned did not participate in the initial distribution.

Oral sources unanimously claim that pastoral clans in the incense territory failed to reach a binding agreement on whether to distribute the frankincense forests for intensive exploitation. The parties involved in the discussion were, on the one hand, wealthy herdsmen with large numbers of stock. They were against formal partition of the area into frankincense fields, since their herds grazed the region in the winter months. On the other hand, in favour of exploitation were two groups with less vested interests in stock breeding. Herd-poor families with insufficient stock to sustain them, who were therefore already dependent upon frankincense collection wanted the allocation to proceed. Allied with this group were merchants who supported the opening up of the traditional pastoral land for intensive gum production, since the frankincense crop was an important export commodity.

This public discord is reported to have been divisive. Many were the cases of brothers and close kin with differing interests who took opposite sides in the dispute. A man with limited stock who aspired to acquire an incense field or fields understandably wanted his brother or other closest kin to obtain the adjoining property. Any amount of persuasion was not sufficient if the brother was a rich pastoralist committed to his herds.

The lack of initial consensus in relation to the distribution and intensive exploitation of a community property subsequently resulted in an inequitable distribution. Rich pastoralists could not finally prevent the allocation of frankincense and responded by declining to obtain their due rights. The consequence of this was the appropriation of the greater and better fields by those with a vested interest in the partition and intensive exploitation of frankincense.

Tenancy and share-cropping arrangements which regulate access to frankincense trees testify to this past unbalanced distribution of customary lineage property. The descendants of those who declined to participate in the initial distribution are now obliged to rent or enter share-cropping arrangements with present owners who inherited rights from their ancestors.

As tradition recounts, if the original holders were either poor nomadic families or local traders residing in trading villages, the present title-holders are mainly fairly rich absentee pastoralists, with a herd size of usually more than a hundred head of sheep and goats and some camels. Some young men start building herds from a few animals they inherit from their herd-poor incense collecting father and eventually succeed in becoming rich pastoralists. Some rich pastoralists lose their animals and turn to cultivating incense. The size of a father's herd is not an important factor in determining the size of the herds of his sons and grandsons. If a father has many sons, the share of the inheritance due to each son becomes limited. Gifts obtained by sons from their fathers when they marry, or their inheritance shares, are important, but environmental factors and occurrence of disease are even more important, in relation to the accumulation of herds among Somali pastoralists. My sedentary father, who had no camel herd since my early childhood, told me that my grandfather was a wealthy camel herder. Some village settlers and migrants to towns are also title-holders.

Among northern Somalis, if a legitimate holder abandons land property, even for a considerable period of time, it is not returned to the lineage for allocation. Nor does it change hands without the consent of the holder as long as he is known to be alive. Abandoned property is used or taken care of by the closest male kin of the absent party. In the case of frankincense, where joint ownership is the pattern, a member of the joint holders over the property may be found in the frankincense region to manage the property.

Tenancy and share-cropping practices are virtually unknown in the north-west agricultural region. Here a pastoralist who wants to settle down or temporarily cultivate a field, obtains a farm on loan from a sedentarised kinsman. The same kinship obligation operates in the pastoral economy and functions to promote the distribution of animals between rich and poor pastoral families.

The pastoral faction which opposed the partition and associated intensive exploitation of frankincense argued that two key objects of economic exploitation (white resin-producing frankincense trees and white milk-yielding stock) are anathema to each other, and therefore cannot harmoniously thrive together in the same environment. Large-scale adoption of gum production was thought to bring havoc to the cherished herds of nomadic people.

The adverse consequences thought to follow the economic transformation, and the lowly position held by collectors in relation to herdsmen, explains the apprehension of the pastoral faction to this change. The consequent limited access to the foliage of the frankincense trees, which is cherished by the animals, and the pastoral resources available in the frankincense fields, may be considered the most important reason for the faction's refusal to cooperate.

The system of frankincense use understandably made some crucial concessions to the dominant pastoral system. Pastoralists retain the right to cut the foliage of their frankincense trees for the animals. Moreover, other than the commercial frankincense species, all usable natural objects that are found in the fields are not subject to prescriptive rights and are free for public exploitation. Despite these concessions, the relations between pastoralists and title-holders, many of whom are pastoralists in their own right, are strained and less harmonious. Some pastoralists cut down branches or fell trees for animals.

Others illicitly remove considerable parts of the bark for the purpose of extracting tannin. These practices either greatly damage the trees or kill them, and may lead to litigation and arbitration between the parties concerned. Pastoralists have the right to graze the frankincense fields, but actual damage to the trees by pastoralists is not allowed. By rubbing their body against the tapped frankincense trees, sheep and goats may knock off the maturing resin from the bark. This annoys the collector.

Frankincense has continued to be produced in the frankincense region of Somalia since antiquity, though perhaps not consistently. However, both local and existing written sources tend to suggest that the actual distribution of the Boswellias in Bari region took place in the middle of the nineteenth century. In the neighbouring Erigavo region the partition seems to have taken place at a later date, in the early decades of this century.

The details of the partition among the easterly Majeerteen clan in Bari region could be established more accurately than could be done for the westerly frankincense-holding clans, the Warsangeli and Habar Toljecla (Isaaq). Majeerteen informants, particularly those who belong to the traditionally aristocratic Cismaan Maxamuud lineage, unanimously state that a revered sultan, clan leader Maxamuud Yuusuf (Hawaadane) encouraged and ceremoniously implemented the partition of the commercial forests.

Durrill's (1986) historical paper on famine in northern Somalia details the successive office holders of the Majeerteen Sultanate in the area. According to this source, Maxamuud Yuusuf, who is said to have affected the partition by informants, appears to be Maxamuud (II), who became the first sultan at the age of 18 in 1855. For reasons unknown the first sultanate, based primarily upon wealth derived from shipwreck, is reported to have consolidated power in 1809.

Durrill's paper shows that the Majeerteen sultanate exerted considerable control over the local productive resources long before Maxamuud (II), who oral sources claim to have implemented the partition. According to the author, "By 1843 Ismaan political leaders operated twelve vessels all but one of which sailed exclusively to Aden and back out of the Majeerteen ports on the north east. From that commerce, Majeerteen merchants accumulated capital and invested it in livestock. In 1843, Cruttenden reported that 'some of the principal Bedouin chiefs' possessed 'upwards of a thousand she-camels' and even more goats and sheep. The chiefs parcelled out herds of fifty to eighty animals to their wives and clansmen, who became clients as well as kin. In addition, Majeerteen traders bought usufruct rights to the country's marble hills where acacia trees grew wild. Earlier, herders had claimed acacia plots held in common by the sultan for their own use at no cost. After 1843, the Ismaan sultanate sold those rights to merchants, which then rented acacia plots to herders in exchange for a portion of the gum crop. Pastoralists became tenants, caring for Majeerteen merchant's livestock and gum trees, although they were somewhat better fed for their trouble than before." (Durrill 1986:296–297).

The cited evidence traces the present share-cropping and possibly rental arrangement practices to the Majeerteen sultanate. The sultan's rights over gum species held in common with the part-time pastoral collectors testifies to the fact. After 1843 there was a transfer of usufruct rights to the local merchants who, in turn, demanded shares in the produce from the dispossessed local pastoralists.

The impact of the sultan's commitment to the export economy has been ably discussed by Durrill. The drive to increase exports of livestock led to a dramatic increase in the number of animals and hence pressure on land. It undermined the traditional subsistence and effective drought management strategies. Moreover it has altered the supplementary economic relations between the pastoralists and coastal fishing communities to the chagrin of the former. The Majeerteen political economy created stratification and relations of economic exploitation. Perhaps most importanly, local pastoralists in the region seem to have lost their ability to weather the drought spells that occur in the area.

To support the history of the aristrocratic lineage, Majeerteen informants claim that sultan Maxamuud (II) partitioned two essential valuables between his subjects. The right to govern was offered to the Cismaan Maxamuud lineage, while the commercial forests were decreed to be justly distributed between abiding subjects residing in the frankincense region.

As a matter of fact, whether the distribution was effected by one of the Majeerteen sultans or not, it has certainly not been justly effected, as tradition reports. Reluctant to participate in the partition because of their commitment to herding, many families were given no rights over the group property to the advantage of the local traders and herd-poor families who were eager to obtain incense fields. Many members of the Cismaan Maxamuud lineage who still live in the region, and others who have migrated to the interior and to towns, still possess rights they obtained at the time of the partition. This contradicts the oral claim that the sultan justly gave this lineage the right to govern, and the other local resource, frankincense, to his poor subjects belonging to other lineages.

Frankincense-owning clans to the west of the Majeerteen, the Warsangeli and Habar Toljecla, like other northern clans, lack a historic authority system comparable to the distinctive Majeerteen sultanate. Partition proceeded in a more conventional form. In the beginning, most of the people were uncertain about prospects of obtaining frankincense forests at the expense of herding. This hesitation gave local traders living in villages and poor herders the early advantage of acquiring many large frankincense fields.

Among the Habar Toljecla in Erigavo district a stampede to obtain large fecund fields followed the partition progress when people realised the importance of owning the property. Dominant lineages within the clan, and within the lineages those families with sufficient strength of adult men to further their interest, took proportionately greater shares of the available community property in relation to the weaker lineages and families.

Most probably, faced with disputing claims over incense fields that were partitioned on the basis of customary means, the colonial administration in British Somaliland compiled a gum and *damas* (Conocarpus lancifolius) register. A hand-written register is still available in the District National Range Office in Erigavo town. It is dated 1937 but quotes an earlier register. It details some interesting information on the types of species that grow in particular fields, the name of the fields and areas in which they occur, and the owning families and their clan affiliation.

It is interesting to note that *damas* plants which grow in the valleys of the incense escarpment, were subject to prescriptive rights in Erigavo region, rights similar to those pertaining over Boswellias. *Damas* plants produced timber for export to Aden before the middle of the twentieth century. Afterwards timber lost its export value and hence people lost interest in excercising control rights over them. This made it easier for the Siyaad Barre government to resume control over the plants. At present those who want to cut down timber for local building, obtain a permit from the district National Range Office, without seeking the authorisation of the previously owning families.

Incense people in Erigavo region recount some useful customary techniques that somehow regulated the assertion of rights over frankincense trees. The person who did the first tapping over the frankincense trees in a particular field in the territory of his lineage, was acknowledged as the legitimate owner. In some cases this principle caused problems. Some initial tappers did not regularly exploit the acquired property to consolidate their rights. Other aspirants who as members of the holding group had claims over the property started to exploit it. The initial tappers and the later exploiters clashed. Such disputes were said to be arbitrated by dividing the disputed property equally between the litigants.

In Bari region it is thought that the sultan sanctioned a tenancy security rule. If a tenant regularly uses the field for a prolonged period without doing damage to the property, and regularly pays the rent, then he cannot be evicted from the field without a good reason. The demand for use by a member of the owning families is an example of a good reason. This important rule does not apply in neighbouring Erigavo region. Nor does it function throughout the frankincense-producing districts in Bari region. Where it seems to partially operate, it may not function without the goodwill of the owners, or the persuasion of an important person such as the local cooperative chairman who is often a respected person in the community.

I tried to find out if some fields were acquired through non-customary means. I found two cases in which frankincense fields were exchanged for wives in Xiis village, Erigavo district. Wives' kin who belonged to different lineages were given ownership rights over frankincense fields by the frankincense-owning husbands.

A different case concerning the transfer of ownership rights to a local merchant creditor in payment of a debt incurred by a client holder has been reported in Galgala village. Another event took place in the same village. A man killed another accidentally. The assailant, who had no male heirs and was a cousin of the victim, offered two fields as some sort of compensation or assistance to the two daughters of the dead kinsman.

The above cases concerning transfer of rights over frankincense in the form of bride wealth, debt or compensation for the loss of a father, are indeed very rare. Moreover, most of these cases are said to have taken place at an earlier time when most of the people were still sceptical about the importance of acquiring the property.

At present, there is virtually no other way in which rights over frankincense could be transferred, other than through male inheritance. In contrast, camels may be sold if necessary. Surplus male camels may be sold in exchange for young female camels that will increase the herd. A female milch camel or a pack camel may reluctantly be given to assist a needy kinsman. Likewise, a plot of cultivable land may be sold, if necessary, by the owner, in contravention of the land laws which prohibit such action.

Certainly joint ownership[1] may be an important factor that helps restrain frankincense property from being marketed. Nevertheless, the resource, which

---

[1] See next section in this chapter.

is unexpandable under the prevailing circumstances, is justly thought of as a long-term investment which is much more valuable than a property that can be offered in assistance to a kinsman, or else exchanged for money. Like cherished camels or agricultural fields, a close kinsman may be given right of use over a frankincense field as a loan, but not ownership rights over jealously-held incense property. Many absentee pastoral families in practice do not utilise the joint property, but the possession of such rights gives them a satisfaction and a sense of security of having a property which is more resistant to drought and therefore one that they can fall back on if they lose their herds.

Multiplication of rights

Of fifty frankincense fields I surveyed in Galgala village, all but three individually-held ones were jointly held by a core of agnatic families. These usually consist of less than ten nuclear families, counting from one to three generations from the original ancestor holder. An incense field known as Sidibhoose which lies near the village can be considered as a typical example. The field was held collectively by the following agnates:

Figure 4. *A case of several agnates collectively owning an incense field*

1. Jibriil Ismaciil
2. Shire Ismaciil
3. Ciise Aw-Yuusuf
4. Cismaan Aw-Yuusuf
5. Siciid Aw-Yuusuf
6. Cali Aw-Yuusuf
7. Xasan Aw-Yuusuf Ismaciil
8. Faarah Xuseen Ismaciil'
9. Maxamuud Ismaaciil

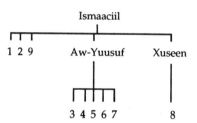

In the example, Ismaaciil is the original ancestor holder of the property. His now elderly sons, Jibriil, Shire (nos. 1 and 2) and Maxamuud (no. 9) are jointly holding rights with the grandsons of their father. After their death, their rights will pass on to their male sons, the same way their dead brothers Aw-Yuusuf and Xuseen passed rights to their living sons (nos. 3–8).

Cases which deviate from joint ownership are very rare. They relate to previously jointly owned property that was divided into small fields individually held by the owning families as a result of disagreement between them. This tendency is more marked in the case of brothers by the same father but different mothers, who are more likely to disagree on the use and management of the joint property.

Very few cases where demographic accident has persistently resulted in a single male heir, starting from the original holder down to the present male holder, account for the second possibility concerning individual ownership over frankincense. Irrespective of its economic advantage in relation to maintaining a balance between an unexpanding resource and potential exploiters, families who do not multiply adequately are considered as

45

unfortunately stricken by a social disaster. It is said that "their fire got extinguished", *dabkoodii wuu bakhtiyey*. This seems to imply that where there is no fire there is no social life and perpetuation of family name.

In general terms, frankincense fields, agricultural land, and camels are idealised as lineage property and hence the prerogative of men. In contravention of the Islamic inheritance rule which prescribes for a woman half the share due for a male, women do not generally inherit the primary resource base of the economic groups in northern Somalia.

The traditional marriage pattern explains the male monopoly of the property of the group. Women generally marry outside the lineage (primary lineage is regarded as an exogamous unit). People say that in extreme cases women may marry members of potential rival groups and possibly non-Somalis, e.g. Somalised Arabs living with Somali clans. Therefore, if women are given rights over important property, they will pass these rights to their children belonging to the husbands' groups.

After marriage women leave their natal group to live with the husbands' social unit. It is the duty of the husband to support his wife and children, and moreover, maintain good relations with his affines. Since women are supported by their husbands after marriage, and by their fathers or married brothers before marriage, it is not thought appropriate that brothers share the father's estate with sisters.

Sedentary cultivators in Borama district evoke sibling sentiment to dissuade women from inheriting agricultural land. If a sister claims or insists on receiving her due rights in her father's estate, it is believed that something terrible will happen, the worst being the death of her brother.

A story about a woman living in Qandala reveals the subtle means men resort to in order to prevent the strongest of women from inheriting frankincense fields. Asha was the only child of her father, and hence expected to inherit her father's fields. The closest male kin of her father, her father's cousin, claimed that women do not inherit frankincense and therefore he was the legitimate heir. Asha fought for the property and tested the strength of both traditional and administrative courts on the issue. Both legal channels are reported to have ruled Asha as the legitimate heir. The male disputant got round the problem by marrying Asha's daughter. Hence in-law relations of marked respect replaced the prolonged feud. In effect, the man obtained access to the property and ensured that his children would inherit the property.

Wives of poor husbands are considerably allowed to bring their husbands to the wife's group and are given use rights over frankincense or agricultural fields. Pastoral women, particularly married ones living with their husbands, may receive token gifts of small stock, a few milk camels or a pack beast from the stock which is inherited from their father. Generally speaking, women may get their due share of the inherited cash. In urban areas they may obtain town property through inheritance or from the money some of them make as government employees or as petty traders.

Collective ownership over a limited and unexpanding property raises the question of how access to property is regulated. The local system which regulates exploitation of the joint property is known as *gaafeysi*, literally "taking turns". This is a system where each member of the right-holding group has a right to exploit the property in turn in a rotating system of seasonal exploitation. For example, if the holding unit consists of three families owning one field, each one will get access to it every third season.

The strict application of the system mainly functions when all the right-holders are on the same economic level, and therefore the exploitation of the joint resource by all is important, for example, when the holding members are all poor. In practice, however, this is quite rare. Often some families are better off than others. These well-off families allow poor families with little stock to regularly exploit the joint property without obligation. In this sense, the property may be said to function as a local social security support scheme for the poorest owning families in the region.

Right-holding poor herding families which obtain usufruct rights from their joint holding kinsmen, are better off than their counterparts who have no rights. Landless herd-poor tenants, who constitute the bulk of the frankincense collectors, rent or enter share-cropping contracts with the right-holders for the exploitation of the traditional group resource.

The management of the joint property is mainly assumed by a member of the owning group who may be residing in the area or in close proximity. The manager is required to have a strong and influential personality. The senior elder of the title-holding families who possesses such qualities preferably assumes the position. The manager shall protect the frankincense stands from pastoral destruction or inappropriate exploitation if the field is worked by tenants. Meditation in border disputes and regulation of use among the right-holders are also his tasks. This status is different from that of the work party leader which is designated by the same Somali term *muqadin.*[2]

The system of seasonally rotating use among the joint holding families as well as having an acknowledged field manager, could be considered as cultural mechanisms that function to try to resolve the disparity relating to the multiple use right over a proportionately limited joint property. The pursuit of alternative subsistence production, such as stock breeding or town employment by some holding families, actually reduces the competition for the use of the property by all the owners. However, such measures do not appear to resolve effectively the imminent ownership crisis which would eventually result from cumulatively increasing rights on unexpanding natural plant property over generations.

Joint holders may relinquish their use right for the benefit of a needy kinsman, but they do not give up their titles, even if they go abroad or to towns in Somalia. A Somali sailor working in Great Britain wrote this letter to the district administration in Erigavo, the former British Somaliland. I found the letter in the gum and *damas* plantation register referred to above. The sailor asks the authority to register properly his incorrectly registered frankincense field.

Presumably the author wanted his mother to look after the field. This may suggest he had estranged his closest male kin who would normally take care of the property of an absent kinsman. Nevertheless, what is important in terms of asserting "ownership" rights is the demand for the name of the migrant to be registered against the real name of his wrongly registered gum field.

---

[2]See chapter four.

28.8.1956
Erigavo

Dear Sir

I have the honour to inform you that the gum plantation which belongs to Ali Bulhan is called *Shela Madow*. Ali Bulhan is a sea man. He was absent from Somaliland in 1926, so his plantation was misregistered by someone else. *Galdameer* is not the proper name for my plantation, but it is the place we put the gum when it is collected.

Its real name is:

a) Meydi "Mantek Yareh"
b) Moxor "Doomo Yareh"

I would be most grateful if you would kindly register the mentioned plantation against my name on behalf of my mother.

Your obedient servant

Ali Moh'd H.Y.

Musa Ismaaciil/Abdulla Hamud

To take an example showing the degree to which multiplication of rights over unexpanding natural frankincense fields can be stretched, I document the case of an extended family I knew in Galgala village. The descendants of the original ancestor holder (grandfather of the present right-holders), now number 70 male individuals who jointly hold 3.5 frankincense fields that were acquired through inheritance. After two to three generations, if male members propagate sufficiently, we will witness a lineage counting four to five generations to the original ancestor, whose male members all claim legitimate rights over their ancestor's property.

It is difficult to speculate how customary or state laws will deal with a tenure system where there are accumulating rights over generations on an unexpanding frankincense property. Despite its limitations, it appears to contradict the current tendency of individual ownership over previously communal land that has been reported for many sedentary societies. In contrast to other cases, it is not viable to parcel out the collective property between the legitimate right-holders. The best option, then, in the absence of conflict, is to maintain the integrity of the collective property.

Utilisation of the frankincense property

The sedentary cultivating families in the northwest mainly reside in permanent settlements often in close proximity to the agricultural land. This is not the usual case in the frankincense land. The possession of frankincense property seems not to have induced permanent settlement of actual owners who regularly exploit the resource. Apart from a relatively small number of village-based collectors, the gatherers are chiefly semi-settled herd-poor tenants who rent the property from absentee pastoral holders.

Frankincense production is relatively speaking less desirable, partly because of endemic exploitation which profits traders more than producers, and partly because it is a difficult task in a difficult environment. Collectors therefore seem to seize the earliest opportunity to change occupation. Those who manage to build up sufficient stock of more than one hundred head of sheep and goats and some camels start raising herds. Others migrate seasonally to coastal towns in the region, or permanently to the larger towns in the country. At the same time, some pastoral families whose herds have dwindled in size and who therefore cannot without hardship subsist on stock breeding, start to cultivate frankincense. Hence, though there may be a fairly stable number of families who engage in collection during a given season, frankincense production is not as permanent as sedentary cultivation or pastoralism in terms of families who regularly exploit the property. Many of the people living in the frankincense-producing districts in Bari region who are now engaged in different activities, have at one time in their life engaged in frankincense collection.

Frankincense collectors make substantial use of the local system which assigns name labels to territorial space. More than the general tendency to give particular names to rivers, streams, valleys, gorges, and other mountain features of the escarpment, frankincense fields are characteristically given particular names. Thus each and every field in the frankincense region of Somalia bears its particular name. In contrast, agricultural farms in the north-west do not in general have specific names though agricultural areas often possess names. Because of the irregular use and the difficulty in maintaining vigilance over the property, one may surmise that it behoves the owners to name frankincense fields. This makes it easier to exert control over distant fields that grow wild but contain commercially valuable frankincense-bearing species. Faced with the problem of parcelling out desolate mountain regions into bounded frankincense fields, incense people may have rightly thought it necessary to delimit collection plots by giving them particular names. Table 2 shows a sample of the names on some frankincense fields taken from a survey of fifty fields made in Galgala village.

A distinctive feature of the field, the quality of the gum resin it produces, the dominant plant population in the plot, or a prominent geographical feature in the site, generally provide grounds for giving particular names for the fields. The name of the field and that of the station are often used synonymously. The frankincense field station in Somali is known as *gole* , "temporary site". It is a pastoral institution (variant *gale*) which designates the temporary sites of the mobile pastoral herd units of the nomads.

The Somali word *xiji* for the frankincense field has various designations. In one sense it applies to the frankincense stands that are exploited. In another context, it seems to refer to the frankincense field as a territorially bounded physical entity. In the most general sense, it is also used to imply Boswellia species that yield gums and resins which have a market value.

Each and every field has a station where incense men reside while working frankincense, store food and harvest incense. Just as no field is ideal without a station, no station is perfect without a track, however treacherous. This mountain track connects the field to a network of tracks which, in turn, connect frankincense sites in an area of production to a village base. Such tracks are frequented by pack camels and donkeys which carry incense and food provisions between rural villages and frankincense collection areas.

Table 2. *Names of some incense fields*

NAME OF THE FIELD	MEANING
1. Dankung	*Dankung* plants are the dominant plant vegetation in the plot.
2. Dhabab	Literally means well-protected. The rock cave station which bears the name of the field is naturally well protected. It is said to be large enough to shelter 400 head of sheep and goats from the rare stormy weather in the area.
3. Huraahur	Can be translated as torrid. Frankincense stands grow in a deep gully which is bounded by towering rock walls that prevent free movement of air, making the site a sweltering place to work.
4. Haama gooye	Literally means cutting off domestic vessels. The track that leads to the field is extremely narrow. To avoid falling into a bottomless abyss laden camels tend to lean toward the protruding vertical rock face. This is likely to knock off water containing vessels carried by the burden camel.
5. Ilo badan	Literally means abundant sources. Frankincense-bearing species grow abundantly in the site.
6. Meeriye	Literally, the one which causes translocation. Frankincense stands are widely scattered in the plot. To tap them the collector continuously moves from one cluster of trees to another, as the name signifies.

Apart from the elaborate system of names for territorial space, other supplementary techniques are employed to make incense fields distinct territorial entities. Concrete landmarks are commonly chosen to act as boundaries that separate adjacent fields. Two fields on the sides of a horizontal or vertical mountain block are said to be separated by *dardar*, "the top surface of the mountain". Other important mountain features that are chosen as convenient boundaries, where they occur are: *jeex*, gullies and other small natural water courses; *tog-weyne*, a valley or any large river; *wado*, tracks used by people and livestock. In the absence of any significant landmark to act as a concrete boundary between neighbouring fields, piles of stones are erected for the purpose.

Landmarks are not easily destroyed or disputed and therefore constitute tangible boundaries; despite this features such as valleys apparently lack precision as boundaries despite being perhaps ten or more metres wide. Natural landmark boundaries function as buffer-zones that separate adjacent fields. The most valuable property found in these natural fields are frankincense trees. If some trees grow in the boundary they are agreed to be equally divided between the owners.

Frankincense owners also classify frankincense fields to different types by names. The smallest viable field is known as *kob*, "minuscule field". These often occur in difficult environments. The terrain may be rough and rugged, the water point may be distant, or the quality of the resin may be relatively inferior. As unattractive property, they were not acquired in the initial partition, and were obtained by latter aspirants who joined the fray after the good fields had been taken up. Other minuscule fields were previously large and fecund fields that were partitioned by the joint owners, mostly due to conflict over the use of the property .

Large fields are known as *macyaan*, "fecund and large fields". They lie in relatively open and less hostile environments, within a striking distance of the water hole, and may produce superior resin. Closeness to a trading village is also another hallmark of a suitable field. These features of an ideal field are discussed and meditated upon by the joint collectors before they finally decide which field to work in a particular season. Intermediate fields of varying qualities lie in between the less desired smaller fields and the larger and better ones.

Incense men have a common sense knowledge about the number of collectors who can proportionately work on a particular field and its capacity of production in an average season. The table below illustrates this. The fields lie near Galgala village.

Table 3. *Estimated seasonal production and labour capacity of selected fields*

NAME OF THE FIELD	NUMBER OF COLLECTORS	ESTIMATE OF THE SEASONAL OUTPUT/KG
1. Dankung	1	200
2. Damberrehe	1	300
3. Naasacad	1	400
4. Gol	2	600
5. Buura dharje	2	500
6. Ceel dibir	2	600
7. Ilo badan	3	700
8. Kashkaash	3	700
9. Xoor xooro	4	1000
10. Booj	6	1500
11. Jeeni dheer	8	2000

The first three fields are typical examples of minuscule fields. They are ideally worked by an individual collector who produces in an average year about 200–300 kg of *meydi* incense if the field grows *yagcar* species, or about twice of this amount if it is *moxor*. The last two fields represent large fields which are worked by a comparatively large joint unit of collectors of 6–8 men. Their production capacity in an average season varies between 500–2000 kg of *meydi* incense.

Estimated seasonal yields may be expressed in camel loads. One camel load is assumed to correspond to 150 kg. A field that produces roughly 750 kg of frankincense is said to yield 5 camel loads.

Despite the commonplace knowledge of estimated annual yields of fields and the number of men who suitably work them, neither tenants nor owners have a knowledge about the number of trees that are found in a particular field at a given time. Tenants do not bother to count the number of trees they visit in a day, although the number depends largely upon the stage of the tapping cycle. In the initial tapping cycles there is less resin to be harvested. According to informants in Galgala village, a man can then visit three times (approx. 150 individual trees) the number of plants per day he can visit during the last cycles when more resin is harvested.

Lack of knowledge of the number of trees in a field does not mean that owners have no effective control over incense property. Trees the bark of which are removed for extracting tannin bear the scars, and branches cut by nomads for animals to graze can apparently be detected. Trees that are removed from their site leave white coloration on the rocky site on which they cling to. Such white stains which are visible from a distance provide sufficient indication for the owner to find out if the missing trees were removed on purpose by pastoralists or others.

Considering the characteristics of prescriptive rights on frankincense property it is interesting to note that the system embodies a fundamental pastoral principle which maintains free access to nomadic resources. Accordingly, prescriptive rights apply only in relation to the major property that is found in the fields, the frankincense-bearing species. Other usable material objects which exist in the fields, such as pasturage, naturally-occurring water and wild fruits, are explicitly communal property. This pastoral predisposition has been ably described by Lewis: "Grazing is regarded as a gift of God to man in general and not as parcelled out amongst specific groups. Pasture thus is not subject to ownership in the ordinary sense, and the right to graze in an area depends upon its effective occupation" (Lewis 1962c:3–4).

In principle, sedentary cultivators in the northwest region possess prescriptive rights over all the usable material objects which occur on their farms. In practice, however, a farmer may not effectively exercise strict control over all the resources. Most commonly he is unlikely to deny kin members of the community the use of naturally-occurring water and pasture existing in the fallow parts of his land. However, he may reserve areas on the fields that grow abundant and better grass for the exclusive use of his cattle and small stock.

Despite significant differences in the frankincense and sedentary landuse systems, they could be said to share an important feature. They tie members of a social unit to plots of land in the territory customarily associated with the group. This economic transformation of previously pastoral groups took place in an equitable form in the northwest agricultural region. All members of the lineage who wanted to become sedentarised obtained fields in the land of the holding group. Because of this landless cultivators may not be found among those who first settled down in the agricultural villages of their group. Currently, pastoral families who belong to sedentarised lineages usually obtain land on loan basis (*maal*, the same way milk camels are loaned to destitute herdsmen by a wealthy pastoral kinsman) from their sedentarised land-holding kinsmen.

In the northeast, an unbalanced distribution of frankincense took place. Frankincense fields were obtained by some members of the land-owning social units at the expense of others who declined to obtain their due rights over the common property. Consequently, the present descendants of the landless ancestors, if they want to exploit frankincense, rent or enter into share-cropping relations with the living offspring of the original ancestor title-holders who inherited rights.

Rental and share-cropping relations obtain between title-holders and landless tenants who in many cases belong to the same *dia*-paying group. At a higher level of grouping, tenants who belong to lineages which proportionately own less property or engage in collection, may rent fields from neighbouring and matrilaterally related lineages with more incense resources. For example, many Sawaaqroon tenants in Alula district rent fields from title-holding members of Cismaan Maxamuud lineage who are their affines, although a great number of them have migrated outside the district. In short, people who stand in such unbalanced relations in relation of access to the exploitation of customary common property are kinsmen.

This is not to deny that, in many cases, permission to exploit freely the joint resource may be given on a consensus basis, or by the authorisation of the acknowledged field manager, to a needy kinsman who falls outside the category of right-holder. In general, it is not kinship morality that primarily regulates access to the exploitation of frankincense property, as shown by the institutionalised tenancy and share-cropping arrangements in the frankincense economy.

Owners and landless tenants who stand in unbalanced relations with respect to the exploitation of the frankincense property, do not totally negate kinship obligations, which operate outside such relations. For instance, right-holders may evict a distantly related tenant from a field to rent it to a closer agnate. Such a move is thought inappropriate and may be restrained by the wider body of kin who disapprove of the act. Also a related tenant may be permitted to pay the rent at the end of the season instead of in advance. If he is unable to pay the rent he may be given a running credit. Nevertheless, if a kinsman openly refuses to pay the rent, or unreasonably delays it, or more seriously damages the property, the right-holders have the right to evict him.

Women do not inherit frankincense, but are not denied the right to exploit the property. Women who are married to poor husbands from a different lineage residing with the wife's group, are assisted by being allowed to exploit the joint property of their male kin. Widowed women raising children may be given the rent proceeds from the fields of kin.

Poor kin who are members of the owning group benefit from kin obligation with respect to the exploitation of the property. In some cases, they are allowed to utilise the property regularly without obligation, paying rent as far as circumstances allow.

Pastoralists, no matter whether they are owners or not, have the right to cut the leaves of the trees for the animals which cherish the foliage of frankincense trees. This important fringe right in relation to the exploitation of the most valuable plant that is found in the region, testifies to the importance of considering different rights that are exercised over the property.

The different rights over the primary property are important for those who exercise it, and give us a wider view of the ways in which the property is made use of. The most interesting aspect of frankincense landuse is that different rules apply to the various material objects found in the fields. In the most general sense, they are indicated by the prescriptive rights held by a core of agnatic families over the naturally-growing commercial forests, and the communal rights over all the other natural useful things that occur in the frankincense fields.

CHAPTER FOUR

Organisation of the frankincense production

A remarkable and distinctive feature in the frankincense economy is that different codes apply to different economic spheres. In contrast to the primarily family-based crop production in the northwest, frankincense cultivation is corporate. The major unit of production often consists of a joint work party of adult men, mainly two or three co-labourers and less than eight collectors, representing their families. Individual members of the work party are thought to contribute equally to the seasonal production input.

The distribution of the seasonal proceeds from the joint effort is rather complex. Here group and individual accounts are kept separately in order to effect an equitable distribution of final output. Investment of production, such as food for work which is consumed by the unit of production throughout the season, is prescribed as collective. The total seasonal investment expenditure is first recouped from the total value of the joint output, the balance is then equally divided between all the members of the unit.

Collateral with these collective economic spheres (labour and production input), is an individual family credit scheme. Each member of the work party is responsible for the credits incurred by his family. This is deducted from the individual's respective share obtained from the final collective proceed.

Thus two economic spheres are distinguished, production which is regulated by a collective code, and domestic consumption where individual responsibility for the family credit is the rule. The system which seems so complex functions to organise group labour which is necessary for frankincense production, while at the same time maintaining a just distribution of the joint labour by requiring each labourer to take responsibility for the credits of his family. This is because credit requirements for the different families differ greatly because of varying needs and different strategies. These different economic patterns will be seen to take place in a social context of economic exploitation between trader creditors and client kin collectors.

Relations of production

In the past, prior to the collectivity experiment initiated by the regime which came to power in 1969, a share-cropping arrangement locally known as *nidaam shaqo*, literally "a system of work" and more precisely "labour code", prevailed as a common scheme. Customarily it regulated economic relations between three kin groups generally belonging to the same *dia*-paying group, frankincense collectors, owners of the primary resource, and local merchants who were the source of credit.

The tripartite system of distribution which was indeed more complex than is usually reported (i.e. in some cases title-holders acted as creditors, or creditors holding rights), dictated the gross value of the seasonal incense produce to be partitioned into three equal parts. One part was allocated to the owners of the means of production. The second portion was allocated to cover production expenditure and went to the merchants who supplied credits usually on hefty profits. And the remaining third was all that left to be obtained by the actual collectors. In the event of joint production, members further divided this share among themselves on an equal basis. The share due to each collector was deducted from the credits incurred by his family. The second type of arrangement was "wage labour", in Somali *maqdac*. A title-holder, or a sub-contractor who rented a field from the owners used to hire wage labourers. Incense labourers received in exchange for their labour a certain amount of incense or some agreed cash. In addition the employer also paid for food consumed while engaged in production, a pair of shoes and two pieces of cloth. The rental arrangement provided a third variant. Tenants rented fields from the owners without entering into a share-cropping arrangement or selling their labour.

In recent times, tenants in a subordinate position vis-à-vis kin owners and merchants have spontaneously started to oppose unbalanced economic relations. The difficulty of finding wage labour or share-croppers, the modification of the traditional share-cropping—where it still exists—and other transformations discussed in chapter seven demonstrate this.

Partly because local traders represented an economic group distinct from rural incense collectors, and partly because the interaction between merchants as a source of credit and client producers was frequent and of most consequence, community poets often spoke of their relations with exploiting kin merchants. Using poetic media as a cultural explanation of the existing relations between the two groups, I want to look into those past relations.

The following anonymous verse was obtained in Xaabo village, Alula district. It demurely points out how the fruits of hard labour are appropriated by an assortment of village kin patrons. The poet uncharacteristically takes the plight of the exploited incense men to Allah, the ultimate judge. In contravention of the religious edict which demands contented acceptance of the predestined condition, the poet suggests why compassionate Allah has not provided them with a more noble and less exploitative occupation.

The first three lines of the verse mention the difficulty underlying the production of frankincense. Then the discussion proceeds on to note the embezzlement of the goods that has caused the producers a lot of trouble. The position of men of religion as accountants literate in rudimentary Arabic is referred to. Such religious accountants and others, such as shop assistants, porters, and intermediaries, are described as an unholy alliance of townspeople who exploit incense people. Most of their services were counted against the collectors.

Tenuously escaping fatal accidents while traversing treacherous precipices
Haunted by the grinding sound of sorghum in the later part of the night
Consoling myself in the face of such grave and potential danger
After I make ready, my produce is finally hoarded in a town store
The one who transported, the other who distributed and yet another who exports
If the turbaned literate man of religion is given the pen
And accounts are set down by the actuary man of religion
My marketed merchandise gets apportioned between nine unholy patrons
Improvised stone unit and unreliable bush scale aggravate our grievances
And we stink like unknown itinerant beggars
Other communities enjoy their respective shares of the predestined noble wealth
To deserve our lowly exploit, oh Allah, are we a low caste without clan affiliation
And may I ask, where is our just share of the distributed community resources?
Certainly the type of wealth we aspire to is apparent to You
I did not mean to question Your just distribution of resources. (7)

Kin merchants and intermediaries are widely accused of having devised measurement units and bush scales with the aim of extorting more incense. To make standard weight units heavier to give false value favourable to the patron, it is reported that some merchants cemented lead weights underneath the standard units. The last section of the verse is a complaint to Allah about the frankincense economy which is projected as lowly and undesirable in relation to the other subsistence economies in northern Somalia.

Informants in Bosaso town told me a story about a dishonest trader who is thought to have died as a consequence of his deceptive practice. As a covert holding back mechanism he tied to the shop scale a string slipped through the wooden counter and long enough to touch the ground. By holding down the string attached to the scale with his toe he was able to get more incense per unit. Eventually the deceiving digit became infected and caused the death of the trader. The event is cited as divine punishment for the dishonest.

Before the latter half of the twentieth century merchants were largely responsible for exporting the incense produced by their clients. This gave them a monopoly over external marketing information which some are reported to have manipulated to their advantage. Declaring lower value for the consigned merchandise is said to have been the practice of some merchants.

A story told in Qandala town testifies to the fact that some merchants jealously guarded external marketing information. For the first time, a merchant was accompanied by some client producers on a trade voyage to India to where *beeyo* incense was exported before Aden developed into a frankincense emporium in the twentieth century.

The merchant devised a ruse to prevent intruding kin-client followers accompanying him to the market. When they arrived at Bombay port, he told them that the place had a stringent sexual rule which obliged any customer want to sell his goods in the market to undergo anal sex before being allowed to sell goods. The trick worked and clients preferred to stay aboard the dhow, entrusting the task of selling the goods to the trader.

In the 1930s, an incense collector in Qandala district was reported to have become insolvent. He could not pay all the debt that had accumulated over the years. His creditor who was his brother-in-law eventually took him to court. The court ordered the auctioning of the property of the indebted. The decision incensed the pauper collector who committed the episode to a short verse. Customarily the brother-in-law must not press hard the brother of his wife let alone take him to court. On the other hand, to compose an abusive poem against one's brother-in-law is not the norm.

> I have no herds that graze the pasture of the rains
> Nor do I export dried fish to import sorghum
> Brother-in-law I have no shops open for me anywhere in the world
> The debt I owe you is not large enough to warrant an invading judicial force
> Leave auctioning my utensils, the world is wayward and fate ridden. (8)

In the past and to some extent still today, clients were given shoddy goods or those that had remained in the store for a long time on loan. The denial of desired goods when needed annoyed incense collectors. Sometime before the Second World War, an incense collector in Qandala district is said to have requested rice on credit terms from his kin patron. He was refused and told to accept sorghum instead. He expressed his rage in this short verse:

> Fellow townsman do not taunt me contemptuously
> Spiced bread freshly served out from the oven
> And good *maanguuri* rice is what you eat all day long
> My ribs are hard pressed by the consumption of sorghum
> Without a grindstone to crush it, it's as bitter as the seeds of *cawaag* tree
> May sorghum forever disappear from the face of the earth. (9)

Some mechanisms of the local system of exploitation explained in this section, bear comparison with those that existed between Aden traders and Somali merchants in Aden prior to current collectivisation. As shown in the first chapter, Aden merchants obliged Somali customers to buy shoddy goods or cleared out old and expired products from trade stores in exchange for their frankincense crop. As we have seen in the above, local merchants sometimes required their kin clients to take poor quality goods on credit. Aden merchants fiddled measurements and charged various services against Somali customers. Local merchants are seen in the above to do similar things vis-à-vis client kin-producers. In this sense, it can be said that local merchants were passing on to their clients some swindling practices to which they were subjected in Aden.

As to the frankincense collectors, the majority of them are adult married men. Unmarried men who collect incense often work not as independent producers but as members of their father's household before marrying and establishing their own nuclear family.

About two-thirds of the actual collectors own only limited stock, mainly between thirty and seventy head of sheep and goats, in some cases a pack camel, but hardly any camel herd. For such families frankincense collection is the mainstay and herding supplementary.

Two principal types of frankincense-gathering families may be differentiated. The prototype frankincense-collecting family is a semi-settled one which habitually herds its limited stock in the frankincense region. This kind of a family is primarily dependent on collection and because the herd is too small to allow mobile nomadism, its members venture beyond the frankincense region only under extreme conditions. Adult men of primarily incense-cultivating families periodically commute between the semi-settled nomadic homestead and frankincense fields. They temporarily reside in incense field stations during the tapping cycles and return to the hamlet at the interval in the frankincense maturing period that occurs between the regulated successive tapping cycles.

Families based in villages that are scattered across the frankincense region form the second type of incense-cultivating families. Not unlike their cultivating rural counterparts, they keep a very limited number of stock in the villages. The herds of those with large stock are looked after by nomadic kinsmen, or a member of the family following the cyclic nomadic movement.

The economy becomes more diversified in villages like Galgala, where small-scale irrigation is practised. Here it is difficult to say which activity is the most important for a family doing a stint both in frankincense collection, herding and irrigated agriculture. When irrigated fruits and vegetables grow well, the proceeds from their sale provide the main source of income. In years with less successful agriculture, more labour is invested in the production of incense, and animals may be sold to cover any shortfall.

Herd-poor semi-settled rural families and village-based collectors seem to account for more than two-thirds of the actual gatherers. The remaining third largely consists of wealthy pastoral families, with herds of more than one hundred head of sheep and goats and camel stock. These rich pastoralists practise migratory nomadism and move between the frankincense region and the interior pasture lands. Because they are less tied to the frankincense region, only those with family labour to spare from herding are likely to engage a member of the family in the production of frankincense.

The cultivation of the *yagcar* species that produces the expensive *meydi* incense, falls for the most part in the autumn cool season, when nomadic families encamp in the escarpment. The strategy is to derive income from frankincense exploitation which is exchanged for food and other domestic goods, to save animals which othewise would have been sold for the purpose.

A local axiom says that two types of families, poor families and families with surplus labour are most favourably placed to exploit frankincense, *xiji waxa ka shageyn kara nin ceydh ah iyo nin ciidan leh*. This implies that herd-poor families have little alternative in a resource-poor region, and are impelled to devote themselves to the intensive work of frankincense cropping, while other families like the rich pastoralists with surplus labour, can make a good income out of it by deploying a free person in the production of incense. It is claimed that someone engaged in another activity would not be able to do properly the intensive and regulated work required in frankincense cultivation.

The majority of semi-settled herd-poor frankincense collectors do not have direct rights over the fields they cultivate. As tenant labourers they obtain access by renting fields from absentee pastoral holders. In the past, both rental and share-cropping arrangements seemed to be common. Currently, the rental arrangement is increasingly displacing share-cropping.

The seasonal rent is known as *cawaaj* in Bari region and *sad* or *haarad* in Erigavo. The word *cawaaj* is used in two contrasting social contexts. In non-formal discourse a man might refer, without constraint, to livestock exchanged for a bride derogatively as wealth earned in exchange for women's reproductive organs, *xoolo cawaaj*. In formal occasions, especially on the occasion of contracting a marriage and agreeing on bridewealth, bridewealth is described as an act of honour, *xurmo*, not an act of buying women's sexual organs.

The word *sad* which is also known in Bari region, connotes a system of distribution in terms of which a group of people allocate something between themselves on an equal basis or else on a pre-agreed quota. In this context, the rent is an amount of payment due to a title-holder as compensation from the tenant for the right to use the property.

Polarisation between the owners and tenants, like the actual producers and local traders, as seen in chapter one, has been a moral issue which commonly provided the pretext for unsuccessful intervention by past governments. Given the failure of the Siyaad Barre government's attempt to abolish the rent altogether, the issue persists as a potential source of conflict.

The right-holders are now setting high rates for the exploitation of their frankincense fields. In 1985, I witnessed the negotiation of a seasonal rent rate in Bosaso town. The parties concerned finally agreed to increase the rate for a large field from 2,000 to 8,000 SoShs for the production season.

Tenant collectors expect a modest rise in rent, following the increase of both the official producer price and that of the informal market in which they illicitly sell part of the produce. It seems that the parallel market is raising expectations and creating confusion. With an eye on the attractive price of the parallel market, the right-holders are accused by tenants of imposing exorbitant rent charges. Moreover, the increase can be a response to the current transformation away from the traditional share-cropping scheme that is comparatively less demanding for the landless collectors.

Rhetoric is used in this conflict between different interest groups. Owners threaten to evict tenants if they refuse to pay high rents, and tenants counter with the possibility of reporting unfair escalation to the authority. Furthermore, in Bari region, particularly in Bosaso district, it is a popular belief that right-holding families who obtain an income by renting their fields to others are punished for doing this. Making an income from undomesticated and customary common property, with little or no capital investment expended in their exploitation, is thought to be tantamount to living on gains derived from sources regarded as unlawful in Islam. In practice, however, this belief has only a limited impact and cannot stop renting.

Obtaining a forbidden return, like renting a public resource provided by Allah for the benefit of the whole community, is considered unclean in a religious sense, *xaaraam*. Being involved in such a business the title-holding families are believed not to increase as satisfactorily as other families who depend upon proper occupations, farming and herding. To substantiate the ideal of slow demographic growth of the right-holders, people cite odd examples of those with many fields but failing to propagate sufficiently.

The same is said about lineages with comparatively substantial frankincense resources which are small in size and strength. Their unfortunate demographic development is said to be brought about by the dependence of many of their families on the extortion of immoral rent.

The belief in a correlation between the acquiring of rent and slow demographic growth is not supported by conclusive ethnographic evidence. Indeed, many families with large and fairly adequate frankincense property experienced favourable growth. In the neighbouring Erigavo district, families and lineages with abundant resources are said to belong to strong families and lineages who appropriated a great proportion of the resources in the initial partition.

The rent rate varies with the type of species growing in the fields. Frankincense fields growing *yagcar* species which produce the expensive *meydi* incense were rented in 1984/85 in Bosaso at 1,000–8,000 SoShs a season, depending on the size of the field, quality of the resin and other attractive qualities, for instance proximity to a village and a water point. *Moxor* -growing fields, which yield the relatively cheaper *beeyo*, fetched about half the rate of those growing most valuable *yagcar*. A third type of frankincense field which grows a mixed population of *moxor* and *yagcar* has an intermediate rate in general, varying with the relative proportion of the species.

The rent institution which acts as a battleground for the interest groups, tenants and owners, varies in different frankincense-producing districts. The rent rate is lowest in Alula district where it has been regulated by the district cooperative movement, albeit with tremendous consequences, as will be seen in chapter seven. A miniature field growing *yagcar* was rented for about 500 SoShs in Alula at the time of the study, compared to about twice the amount in neighbouring Bosaso and Iskushuban districts.

Capacity of production, and the type of species chiefly determine the rent for a particular field. Other important factors are the proximity of the field to nomadic hamlet or village base (owners of distant fields sometimes rent these out abd cultivate their nearby fields), the distance to the nearest water point, and the physical terrain—open and less rugged sites are preferred to treacherous localities.

Apart from the rental arrangement which accounts for the most common form of exploitation, share-cropping and direct exploitation by individual members of the right-holders constitute the major types of frankincense exploitation. If all the owning families are keen to receive the rent proceeds from the collective property, then it is distributed between them on a rotational basis, the same way that direct exploitation is regulated. However, this is not common and the benefits are often allowed to go to the poorest most needy family.

The frankincense stations

Each collection area or frankincense field has a gathering station. This is known as "temporary residing place", *gole*. Physically the station is a rock shelter located at the bottom of one of the valleys or gullies that cross-cut the area. There are frankincense stations said to be large enough to give refuge to hundreds of sheep and goats during storms. These are distinct from the numerous public mountain caves in the region by being called after a particular field.

Persistent use has made the stations fit for human occupation. Some of them are protected with flimsy pole walls which are strengthened with a thorn fence and have a lockable entrance. Such scant protection is particularly useful nowadays to keep away swarms of monkeys which in some areas have acquired the habit of stealing food from the stations. As a precaution against seasonal and occasional flash floods, the stations are often located slightly above the floor of the valley. The rocky surface above is also terraced to divert run-off water.

It is important that each station be connected to a network of tracks that ultimately connect the fields in an area of incense production to a village base. Donkeys and pack camels frequent tracks where motor transportation is absent.

They transport goods between frankincense fields and rural villages connected to the coastal towns.

Frankincense stations are multi-purpose institutions. They are places of abode for the unit of production while working incense. Almost all keep their rations there, and many store harvested resin in well-protected parts inside the station, though others store their goods in uninhabited caves that are abundant in the region. Of no lesser importance it acts as a social nightclub where neighbours assemble during nights to discuss matters of importance, or indulge in poetry.

The concept relating to a temporary site, the station, is a pastoral one. Camps of different stock residing in a region of grazing at a particular time frequently change sites. The camel camp, *gole geel*, the cattle camp, *gole lo'* and horse camp, *gole faras*[1] are all stock units that frequently change sites under the management of adult herders. Frankincense collectors return to the nomadic hamlet for a rest period which occurs between one harvest and the next. Apart from this temporary evacuation, there is hardly any other evidence to support the assumption that frankincense stations are temporary, other than the fact that Somalis draw heavily from the nomadic culture.

Some features of the frankincense station designate its sedentary characteristics. As a consequence of a prolonged use, the surroundings of some of them are severely denuded of firewood which is essential for cooking and making bonfires in the cold winter months. The occupants of such sites travel an hour or more to get firewood.

Apart from the main fire place that lies inside the station, some sites have another "specialised fire place", *xurfadda kimista*, the fire place for making bread just outside, for baking the staple flour bread that is known as *ruub*, "flour bread baked inside the ashes of a fire". Moreover, some of them, have ground mosques which are marked with stones near the station—a visible symbol of a place frequented by Muslim devotees.

The instruments of production

Instruments used for frankincense cropping are very limited. They consist of three primary tools: *mingaaf*, the scraping knife; *koley*, a large receiving basket; and *dhuraad*, a small carrying basket.

The tapping instrument *mingaaf*, is the most important tool of an incense man. It consists of a wooden handle with a narrow portion, the grip, so designed to protect the knuckles from striking the bark while administering incisions. Fitted at the two ends of the handle are two specialised blades. One is sharp and kept in this condition, as the occasion demands, by rubbing it against a sharpening device. The other blade is quite blunt.

The sharp blade is used for administering incisions along the bark of the trees or scraping off the coagulated resin ready for harvest. Unlike the sharp blade which is used to harvest superior resin that matures along tapped receptacles on the bark of the plants, the blunt blade is a gleaning device. It is used to scrape off droplets of low quality incense that flow along the bark outside the tapped incisions.

---

[1] Because of the decline in the traditional importance of the horse in clan warfare, raising horses has decreased in modern times.

The blades are made of iron, and are processed by local smiths. At the time of my fieldwork, the price for making the two blades necessary for the *mingaaf* was 200 SoShs in Galgala village. A careful incense man prepares two *mingaafs* for the season, although the possession of a single *mingaaf* is not in itself a major obstacle to start working incense. Shaping the wooden handle as well as cutting its narrow protective grip are commonplace skills that are performed by most adult men.

The tapping instrument must not be warmed up or brought into contact with fire. A heated tool is claimed to have a disastrous effect on the frankincense plants. It can kill those trees tapped with it. As a result of this, not only must old instruments be keenly protected from fire but also new ones must be cleansed from the impact of the processing fire. This is done by gashing the new instrument, a number of times, into the trunk of non-commercial resin-producing plants. It is difficult to say if this is some kind of taboo or whether there is a scientific explanation for the behaviour.

In addition to the tapping instrument there are two collecting baskets used in the gathering. The smaller one, *dhuraad*, is very light and can be carried by collectors with the scraping knife while harvesting incense. The incense gathered in the smaller basket is emptied into the larger basket as soon as it gets filled up. At the end of the working day members of the unit of production return from the field carrying the larger basket which contains the day's harvest.

Weaving baskets fall in the domestic sector of activity that is thought proper for women. In Galgala village, incense men usually pay women 200 SoShs for making a basket, though some wives prepare baskets for their husbands. Quite often pastoral women and poor women in the villages make baskets to earn an income. The baskets are made of fibre derived from a rare species, *caw*, Hyphaene thebaica.

Since frankincense is a sticky substance those who handle it require some sort of protective gear. The work uniform of incense men is locally known as *malwaha xijiga*, "the uniform for the production of frankincense". It consists of three pieces of cloth: a loin cloth or short trousers, a shirt or some form of under cloth, a pair of shoes and a head scarf. The uniform is required to fit tightly to the body of the men, especially those who work in treacherous sites. If it is loose there is a danger of it catching a rock snag which may result in a disastrous fall from a precipice.

Although the uniform is rarely washed, it is said that the locally available detergents are powerless to satisfactorily cleanse the resin stains that accumulate on the uniform. In poetry the filthy uniform which is characteristic of incense workers is a point rival poets denigrate in the verbal battle for excellence between antagonistic economic groups.

Despite its ghastly appearance the resin-soaked uniform is claimed to perform a hygienic function. The incense dirt suffocates vermin and thus prevents vermin infestation. Despite the coarse texture and the unpleasant look of the accumulated dirt, it does not smell bad, for after all the resin stain is aromatic.

Organisation of labour

Working with frankincense is a male activity. This verse, by an incense collector poet in Alula district, makes the point clear. It is a response to colleagues who tried to persuade Axmed to compose a dissuasive verse for women who took up incense collection at a critical dry period in the past.

> Honourable Saalax, I explain the issue to you
> I have grown out of teenage and early foolish behaviour
> I am too old to indulge in *dhaanto* dance
> I am a man whose beard has grown fully and attained maximum height
> How could I ridicule my own sisters and Dhudayar
> Hurt them and imperatively stand in front of their faces
> The drought has turned all mankind into hyenas
> People are falling over any place that has any valuable sap
> Scrambling up incense trees, sweltering heat, and eventual disappointment
> Resin sticking to their hairs which cannot be avoided
> The lot of frankincense collection will soon be abandoned as they get plenty
> May Allah provide a better alternative, they will never do with incense. (10)

The poet refused to be persuaded by his friends to defame women with unjust cause. They were impelled to venture into the men's domain of frankincense collection by drought and acute scarcity, which had been worsened by events in the Second World War that affected import. The poet claimed that it is immoral to insult women who are described as sisters and partners of men in general. The role reversal is assumed to be a transient episode. Women would gladly cease working incense to resume their domestic tasks as soon as conditions returned to normal.

Women are responsible for supplementary activities, such as weaving collection baskets and preparing the goat-skin water vessels which are commonly used in the frankincense region. If the nomadic hamlet is encamped in the vicinity, they usually relieve men from fetching water and wood and preparing meals. If necessary, they also keep vigil over the harvested resin which is stored in the rock caves.

The mechanism of tapping is quite simple and can be acquired at an early age. Boys younger than fifteen years can be proficient in administering incisions. The skill is acquired by observing adult men do the task without any formal training.

Frankincense collection is a family enterprise. Most of the unmarried adults who perform the task do so as members of their father's household where they remain until they marry and establish their own nuclear family.

There are two forms of labour organisation. The first and most common is a joint unit of production, containing two, three or four, sometimes more, but usually less than eight co-labourers. Traditionally the most influential member of the unit assumed a leadership role *muqadin*, "work party leader". He had contact with the village traders who were the source of credit, and therefore he mediated between traders and actual collectors. However, he had little authority to impose his will, and his responsibilities never relieved him of the collection work. This status which has changed very little is at present dubbed as the "leader of the unit of production" in the jargon of collectivisation.

The second and less common form of labour organisation is the individual labourer who works a miniature incense field that has the capacity to accommodate one man's labour in a given season. People have a clear understanding of the correlation between fields and the size of the unit of production they can accommodate. Nevertheless, this is not strictly adhered to in practice. It is not uncommon to find a field which is claimed to accommodate two or three working men, being cultivated by one or two collectors.

Team work has certain advantages compared to the activity of an individual collector. It has labour flexibility in terms of allocating necessary tasks. For example, four collective labourers may distribute the tasks in hand as follows: three of them collect incense, while the fourth carries out regular chores, fetching water and fire wood, preparing meals and taking cooked food to workers in the field. Other rare instances when men perform women's tasks include the construction of lineage wells by able-bodied members of the group in a place that is distant from the area where the agnatic hamlets are congregating at the time. In contrast, the companionless individual collector not only misses the comfort of group work in production areas that are less frequented, particularly in the hot *xagaa* season, but also various routine activities easily distributed in team work demand vigorous effort on the part of the individual gatherer.

The individual collector has no choice but to abandon his work, however temporarily, if he must attend to an important matter in the homestead. The consequence of disruption in the production of incense is disastrous since regulated tapping is essential. In the case of group work, temporary absence of one member of the team may not necessarily lead to disruption, even though the tempo of the work will be affected.

With these evident advantages it is no wonder that collective work is the dominant form of labour organisation in frankincense production. Despite its structural persistence the social composition is often mobile and less stable. Membership of one particular unit of production changes from one season to the next. There is a continuous realignment and regrouping between work units in a particular area of production.

Of course there are exceptions to the general social mobility of the joint unit. The most stable unit consists of a father and his adult sons. The unit may also consist of brothers and cousins, but most commonly it is made up of agnates who belong to the same *dia*-paying group. Some agnates as members of a joint party remain together for a number of successive seasons, developing and maintaining trust by working together.

There are several reasons for the social mobility of the work party. Theoretically, all members are expected to contribute equally to the joint venture. This hardly works out in practice. Some members may be more committed to work than the others. The dissatisfaction held by diligent workers against less able or dishonest co-labourers is indicated by a popular saying in Galgala village denigrating those who pretend to be sick in order to abstain from work: "I hate those with a healthy appetite to eat greedily, and at the same claim not fit for work".

Authority is an important factor that can destabilise the collective unit. There has always been an acknowledged leader of the unit. Besides the status which is conferred by the responsibility as an intermediary between the unit and the wider social structures, the leader lacks the power to enforce unpopular decisions. In practice he is not entitled to privileges unknown to others. Relations may go awry if the leader tries to exempt himself from regular work. Frequent absenteeism, and unreasonable excuses which are thought evasive, provide grounds for opposition and may subsequently cause the dissolution of the unit in the next season.

If crucial disagreement on work ethics arises in the middle of the season, an effort is made to minimise a precipitate dissolution. On the one hand, it is not easy to do improvised calculation before the end of the season, so that the available joint output could be distributed between the dissenting members, or to work out the right share for a dissenting member. On the other hand, in general, there are customary rules that promote the unity of the group, at least during the season of production. Individual members who decide to abandon before the last harvest cycle ought to relinquish any claim in the collective produce. The unit on its side must not demand any compensation for the food consumed by the dissenting member with the group before withdrawal.

I was told of several cases where diligent collectors stopped collaborating with the unit. Regardless of the customary prescription, and especially if the departing member has a legitimate cause, some sort of agreement is usually reached. Either some incense is given from the joint stock if the harvest is large, or the disputant relinquishes a share, if the stock is small. Afterwards he may not leave the residing station, and may continue to work a specific part of the joint field. He will assume full responsibility for his expenditure and labour.

Solidarity functions in two major ways in the system of joint production. First, there is the element of collective labour where members equally participate in the production process. Second, the food consumed by the unit in the course of production and related production expenditure, is a collective responsibility. At the end of the season this joint production expense is deducted from the gross value of the joint output.

In contrast to the collective pattern in the sphere of production, domestic consumption is fundamentally individual. Each member of the unit bears responsibility for the subsistence credit obtained by his semi-settled nomadic family during the season. This is paid from the respective shares collectors obtain from the value of the joint produce, after the collective investment is recouped.

In effect, two parallel credit accounts are kept for the producers: the collective credit scheme which covers joint production expenses, and the individual family subsistence credit. The underlying rationale for this is not difficult to perceive. The families of those who constitute the work unit of production naturally have different subsistence requirements. Large families necessarily need more food and other essential domestic goods than smaller families.

Local terms for the two accounts *raas* and *minkiise* clearly express the different patterns. The former term means literally "hearth" and connotes collective sharing of the food communally consumed, while the other term which translates literally as "everybody from his own pocket" designates the individual consumption pattern of the family.

By embodying collective and individual economic patterns in the production and domestic consumption domains, the frankincense economy stands distinct from other economies in northern Somalia. Apart from inter-family cooperation in harvesting, and maintaining some water systems in the northwest, the nuclear family is the chief unit of crop production. Family labour is utilised in the production of sorghum and in raising stock units of cattle, sheep and goats, which represent a supplementary activity of great importance.

Besides some institutionalised and obligatory forms of cooperation, informal cooperation between co-labourers residing in the same frankincense station is of considerable importance. It is not uncommon to use a beast of burden, say a camel or a donkey, belonging to another person in the group for a common end. Someone's cooking utensils may be used in the same way. A tapping instrument is borrowed if one's own tool gets broken and someone else has a spare one.

Cooperation and assistance also occur between neighbouring agnates residing in the stations in an area of incense production. The unit usually borrows food from neighbours when its food is exhausted and it is waiting for a supply to arrive from the village base. Pack animals and tools of production are also borrowed across work parties. Water for preparing food is provided freely or loaned in areas of acute scarcity.

In terms of labour, two types of recruitment methods are distinguished. One is short and friendly assistance offered by those who have finished their work to those who still have a task to complete. This is differentiated from *macdac*,"wage labour"; an incense collector who has an urgent duty to attend to may contract a labourer for a short period, say two weeks. The daily wage for casual labour was 200 SoShs in Galgala at the time of my field work. In Erigavo district, it is reported that seasonal labourers are contracted for frankincense cultivation for an agreed payment, although the system seems to be disappearing.

The production process

The work party consisting mainly of agnates has taken shape and the particular frankincense field they want to exploit has already been jointly decided. Tools of production and other prerequisites are made ready at hand. Food for the labouring party has been transported to the stations. A supplicatory feast, *ducada xijiga*, marks the beginning of the cropping season. This is held in the frankincense stations. Rice is cooked, bread is baked, and sometimes a goat may be slaughtered. In addition there is also some popcorn and coffee.

In the past, people say, the initiation feast was more pompous and brought together a large group of people working in neighbouring fields. Although very few work parties at present perform together, the feast is still popular, and food prepared in different stations is partaken with other incense men and passers-by. The aim is to supplicate a bumper crop and a smooth working season.

General slackening of the beliefs and practices of the community, including the reduction in the initiation feast, is raised by elders as a causal factor for some of the unfortunate things that happen. Events like fatal accidents caused by falling from cliffs attempting to reach trees that grow in treacherous places, diminishing rainfall, and dwindling yields due to over-exploitation, are claimed by elders to be a consequence of lack of respect to traditions by young people, who do not meticulously perform observances as their forebears did.

The feast can be said to be supplicatory. It does not on its own have the power to bring the desired end, the multiplication of the crop. More accurately the performance seems to act as an acceptable venue which could bring about the desired result. After the meal the following prayers are commonly read:

May Allah bestow his blessing *baraka* in the fruits of the working men ... Amen
May Allah protect us from fatal accidents, venomous snakes and noxious creepers
that abound in the area ... Amen
May Allah realise the aspirations of incense men and all good Muslims ... Amen

In Bosaso district, the role of popcorn in the feast is rather interesting. It acts as an augury, although its interpretation is often disputed. If an unacceptable proportion of the popcorn goes bad, perhaps because of improper firing or some other reason, sceptics interpret this as a sign of a poor harvest to come. Others dispute this and rightly blame the method of preparation. However, at the end of the season, if output falls short of expectation, sceptics revive the argument. They say that the augury was a clear indication of a poor harvest. This has not been a blessed field to cultivate, and should have been changed in the beginning, they suggest.

Tapping consists of administering incisions on the body of the frankincense trees where the bark can withstand the wound. The depth of the incision depends upon the depth of the resin-bearing ducts of the plant. The initial cut is no more than a scratch. From small scratches the cuts develop to wider and deeper wounds as the tapping cycles proceed. At the height of the season, the average depth of the cuts may measure about 2.5 mm or more and about the size of the palm of a hand.

Apart from other factors such as the conditions of the plants, the number of tappings usually correspond to the age of the tree. Some of the fecund and large trees may bear about a hundred wounds at a time, while smaller trees that are being tapped for the first time may bear no more than four incisions. Between these extremes lie all sorts of trees that can bear various number of gashes. In general, average trees bear about twenty to forty incisions at a given time.

Tapping is a simultaneous process that involves dual acts. It involves cleansing the wound by exposing the resin-bearing ducts for further exudation. This is done by scraping off from the healed wound the hardened resin or the incense crop from the preceding tapping.

The production of frankincense is based on regulated successive tapping cycles. When men finish harvesting the resin from the previous tapping cycle, they return to the nomadic hamlet or village base to spend the time the resin takes to metamorphose into real hard resin.

The regulation of the cycles is very important. Failure to conform to the rhythm of the cycles could have an adverse effect on production. The initial five or three tapping cycles in the exploitation of *yagcar* and *moxor* species are known as the preparatory cycles. Yield is low and quality of the resin is poor compared to the latter cycles. However, they are necessary to stimulate the trees for increased production in the succeeding peak cycles.

If the plants are not tapped at the right time, the wound may totally heal. Since it takes time to prepare the plants to produce adequate and superior resin, starting the process all over again will cause the negligent collector a great loss, incense men claim. The first tapping incision is known as *calaamad* which corresponds to "marking". Since it is no more than a scratch and hardly any resin is harvested from it, in some areas, it is not counted as a tapping cycle.

The preparatory cycles are referred to as preparing or making the plants produce milk (resin). Because the resin harvest is small, and the act of cleansing or harvesting the resin can be done faster than latter peak cycles, incense men have a longer rest period in the hamlet at these initial stages of collection.

After the preparatory cycles, production and therefore the work that has to be carried out in the fields increases. Consequently, incense men stay for longer periods in the stations.

The last cycle is called *Jadar-goyn* which literally means "harvesting long *meydi* tears" and implies the closing of the season.

Some of the resin exuded by the frankincense plant coagulates on the wound receptacle, while part of it actually flows down along the bark. The resin that hardens on the receptable is harvested in each cycle while the run-down resin is allowed to form valuable long tears, in the case of *meydi* production, to be obtained in the last closing major harvest. In the case of *beeyo* production, the resin does not usually flow, and hardens on the receptacle where it is scraped off into collecting baskets in every tapping cycle.

Thus, in the exploitation of *yagcar* species which produces the expensive *meydi* incense, production consists of one major harvest at the closing cycle and cyclical harvests where the resin that coagulates on the wound is obtained. In the exploitation of the *moxor* species which produces the *beeyo* incense production is cyclical.

Further differences in the exploitation of the two species concern the length of the season they are cultivated. *Yagcar* trees are ideally exploited for a period of about ten months, starting from about the end of August or early September until June the following year. During this period the trees are visited or tapped twelve or thirteen times. *Moxor* trees are, in turn, exploited for about eight months, from about March to October. This ideally constitutes nine or ten tapping cycles.

Apart from some diligent and hard-working men, most collectors do not often complete the ideal tapping cycles for the species. In the case of *meydi* production, a shorter season of eight or nine cycles is very common. Late start, early closing, and of most consequence for production temporary cessation of the work, accounts for the difference.

The effect of weather is explained to be largely responsible for most of the differences in the exploitation of the two species. Hot weather is thought congenial for the production of *beeyo* incense. Hence the tapping of the *moxor* species commences in the short hot season of *kaliil* that occurs before the *gu'* rainy season which starts at about April. Although rain is required to improve the condition of the plants and indirectly increases production, rain water can wash away the *beeyo* resin more readily than *meydi* resin.

Gu' rains, which are unreliable in the frankincense region where autumn rains are important, fall before the succeeding hot season or *xagaa* which marks the peak period in the production of *beeyo* incense. The incense produced in this hot season is superior and is known as the *xagaa* crop.

This high quality *xagaa* crop is differentiated from an inferior fringe crop which is called "autumn crop", *beeyo deyreed*. Made damp and more sticky by the cool autumn weather (October–January), this inferior crop is said to be heavier than the superior but lighter *xagaa* crop. Some collectors are said to mix the two crops discreetly in an attempt to obtain more income from the crop.

Those who labour in the wrong season to collect an inferior autumn crop are not considered professional *beeyo* producers. They are described as amateurish. They are mostly village vagabonds and others forced to make some income from the pursuit.

The cool weather that is thought to have an adverse effect on the production of *beeyo* incense, on the contrary, is held to be congenial for the production of *meydi* incense. Its production peak occurs in the less torrid cool autumn season *deyr*. The cool weather at the time and the fact that the region is populated by nomadic families at this time of the year affords better conditions than working *beeyo* incense in the corresponding hot season of *xagaa* when the region is desolate of life.

This main *meydi* crop is known as autumn crop, *xeysimo sarac*, in Alula district, which is renowned for its superior *meydi* incense. It takes a period of about ten months involving twelve successive cycles. A very rare crop known as *xagaa sarac*, *xagaa* crop, is also reported in the same district. It takes a longer period to produce this latter crop. The rare crop is described as the most intensive form of incense production. The aim is to achieve maximum annual output. Therefore apart from the longer period (one complete year) other important prerequisites must be considered for effective use. It is important that the collectors be free from other responsibilities to allow maximum labour input. To make investment worthwhile the field must be fecund and of the required size to accommodate the labouring party. Frankincense trees must be in good condition, preferably having rested for a period of two or more years.

It takes a period of about 25–30 days for the *meydi* incense to mature. The corresponding period for *beeyo* incense is 15–20 days. The difference is explained in terms of the seasonal variation of temperature. Since the cultivation of the former takes place mainly in the cool season, it takes the resin a little longer to harden than the *beeyo* incense which matures earlier due to the influence of the hot weather of the *xagaa*.

Two alternative strategies are commonly utilised to implement the day's work. One is called *gelin soof*. It literally means "setting out for grazing half day". This is a two-shift system in which incense men work before noon and in the afternoon, with a midday break. The second strategy is also a borrowed pastoral concept and is known as *maalin gaal*. It means "the longest distance covered by a moving nomadic hamlet in a day". No midday break is taken in this intensive labour system which is employed when more work is required to be performed.

If the frankincense trees growing in the field are widely dispersed, as they usually are, the work team splits up into individual collectors labouring in contiguous areas. If the trees grow densely, then they advance abreast to avoid missing some of the plants.

Compared to other economic activities in northern Somalia, frankincense collection seems most intensive. The tapping cycles are synchronised harvest periods that require the necessary work to be carried out at the right time. For more than half of the production season, 4 to 5 months, incense men stay in the fields separated from their families. They have to bear the discomfort of the separation and working in a difficult environment. In the hot season of *xagaa*, *beeyo* collectors have to carry water all the time as a precaution against thirst which can easily kill a man without water.

In this hot season, the desolate and seasonally vacated frankincense region is also pest-ridden. Swarms of small mosquitoes *dhabcad* vex incense men at work. Venomous creepers must also be avoided during the day, and during the nights they pose danger in the rock exposed shelters.

Some perilous surfaces where incense men labour are very slippery. Collectors take off their shoes to minimise the danger of skidding down a cliff.

Despite all possible precautions, sometimes the worst happens. In Alula district alone, five men were reported to have died after falling from precipices in 1983/84. Although this particular season could be considered as unfortunate and exceptional, hardly any season passes without its toll of fatal accidents or death.

Some adverse tapping practices are acknowledged by the collectors. The first is known as "deferred tapping" *caddaal* which is claimed to have a disruptive effect on the regulated production. According to informants in Galgala village, delaying harvest for more than 2 days cannot be immediately corrected.

Precipitate tapping *ceyriin sarc*, literally "harvesting raw resin" is another noxious form of exploitation. Deferred tapping is usually explained as a foible of less committed and lazy collectors, albeit that it may sometimes be caused by extraneous factors. Precipitate tapping is, in turn, said to be employed by avaricious collectors who think they can increase output by administering tappings before the resin is mellowed and ready for harvest. One informant in Bosaso town commented on such misguided behaviour. He compared incense trees exploited in this way with a milk camel from which the herder callously tried to obtain more milk by striking it hard on the udders.

Precipitate tapping is claimed to be harmful to the plants and does not increase production. Most damaging to the plants is an illicit and noxious tapping technique which is called *jaqeyn*, literally "stabbing the tree". Two deep parallel cuts are administered on the surface of the ordinary tapping incision. These extra piercing cuts are rewarding in the short term. Trees slashed in this way produce increased resin, though the effects of damaging their internal organs are disastrous. The plants may die, and even those which withstand the noxious deep cuts take a long time to recover from the impact. Deep incisions are also thought to act as a medium which allows wood borers to infect the trees, a condition which may result from the weakened resistance of the plants.

Another presumably restricted illicit harmful practice is reported in Galgala village. The white peel that covers the bark of the trees is burned. This increases the yield but the trees whose resin is milked out in this way are known to die eventually.

The technical information presented here concerns selected patterns which are intended to represent substantial folk knowledge on the exploitation of the Boswellias. The information, particularly concerning noxious tapping techniques, has social implications as well. In reality the damage done to the trees by the application of inappropriate tapping techniques is tremendous. Perhaps no less than half of the frankincense plant population is to some degree damaged. Tapping scars on the trees that fail to heal after the bark has been inappropriately removed testify to the tendency.

Nevertheless, to explain the damage as a result of deficient and unscientific traditional tapping methods, as technocrats are quick to assume, is very simplistic. Incense men are clear about good and bad tapping techniques and the adverse effect noxious tapping practices have on the plants.

The exploitation of the frankincense forests involves different interests, those of the absentee pastoral right-holding families and tenant collectors. It is the concern and responsibility of the former group to oversee the exploitation of the resource and therefore reduce or forestall any damage. However, these are not often in a position to carry out such a course of action since they are present in the region for only part of the year. Consequently, the damage to the trees which may be caused by some irresponsible tenants for yield maximisation is sometimes detected too late to contain it.

Customary regulations which ban noxious techniques are relatively ineffective to withstand the tendency. That the problem is sociological rather than technical is illustrated in the case of a dispute between the right-holders and the tenants. If the latter feel antagonised, i.e. perhaps threatened with unreasonable eviction, or required to pay high rents, some of them are reported to resort to harmful exploitation so as to inflict economic sabotage as a revenge.

The protection of these commercial local forests is a crucial issue for all those concerned, but I think attending to the social causes of the problem can have a more effective impact than the prevailing tendency which often puts the blame on the local system of exploitation.

CHAPTER FIVE

Non-industrial uses of frankincense

Practical uses of frankincense

Domestic exploitation of the trees

Frankincense has various local uses, although it is essentially an export crop. One minor use is as a source of energy. Collectors abandon the nomadic hamlet to stay in the frankincense mountain-cave stations during the tapping cycles. If the need arises, incense tears are burned inside the dark rock-cave at times during the night. The bright flickering flames of burned incense sufficiently illuminate the cave lodging for most practical purposes. To date, this is an emergency practice resorted to only occasionally, for example to locate vermin in the darkness, in the absence of other sources of light. It is not economical to use a large amount of the expensive frankincense as a source of light energy. The assertion that the practice was more frequent in the past than the present testifies to the current adoption of widespread modern sources of light in the remote areas of incense production. In modern times flashlights and to some extent paraffin lamps are commonly used by collectors.

The kind of incense preferred for occasional illumination inside the frankincense cave-station is of *meydi* quality. It emits a steady bright light comparable to candlelight. It is more suitable than *beeyo* for the purpose, since the latter bursts into mass flame and smoke when burned. The inflammable property of incense is recognised to the extent that passengers aboard trucks carrying incense goods are banned from smoking.

Finally, small incense balls are sometimes used domestically as fire-making catalysts. If the available fire wood is damp from rain, fire-making can be made easier by throwing incense balls into the fireplace. Incense instantly bursts into flame and helps the wet wood to catch fire.

The leaves of frankincense trees provide good fodder for livestock. Camels browse the foliage comparatively easily, since they have long necks and can reach the branches of frankincense trees. The comparatively tiny goats who otherwise could not reach the upper leaves grazed by camels, ascend to bewildering heights on precipitous mountainsides, where the bulky camel cannot go. Standing on hind legs, they graze the low lying foliage of the bigger frankincense trees. The leaves of the seedling and smaller trees are devoured by all livestock species, camels, sheep and goats.

From the bottom of a rugged mountain in the frankincense region, the panorama of goats and sheep grazing on the heights is rather picturesque. Sheep and goats appear as tiny white spots scattered across a rocky surface covered with green leaves of frankincense and other types of plant vegetation.

Perhaps more devastating than the tolerated customary grazing rights over frankincense trees growing in territorially bounded incense fields, is the drastic defoliation, sometimes carried out by ruthless pastoralists. During the *jiilaal* dry season and more so in recurrent drought years, trees are illicitly defoliated or cut down, to fatten beasts incapacitated by drought or disease.

The animal's liking for the leaves, and sometimes the opportunistic destruction of the branches by some nomads for fattening up some of the stock even in good years, can be explained by the fairly high nutritional content of the leaves. The young leaves contain 7% protein, 3% oil, 45% carbohydrates, 25% fibre, over 3% calcium oxide and 0.3% phosphorus pentoxide, and are therefore highly nutritious (United Nations Technical Assistance Programme 1952:202).

The desire of many "owning" families and the government's pretension to protect the commercial Boswellia forests is superseded by an overarching pastoral concept[1] that regulates range resource as "God-given" and fundamentally community property.

The tannin content of the bark of incense trees allows another common form of exploitation that further accentuates the destructive tendency to overexploit these commercially valuable forests. The protective bark is stripped off to dye and disinfect milking and water vessels of the household. Traditional vessels wood-carved or made of plant fibre are thought to require periodical tannin treatment. In the frankincense region, the treatment consists of burning the bark of the frankincense tree inside a hole in the ground. The vessel to be treated is turned upside down and placed over the mouth of the hole, so that its inside is smoked by the ascending smoke. Once the inside is dyed and disinfected, the same is done on the surface of the vessel which eventually assumes a reddish tinge.

Frequent tannin application for the traditional milking and milk storing vessels is thought necessary. Housewives and unmarried daughters who perform such domestic tasks are careful not to cleanse these traditional vessels with water unless absolutely necessary. To do so will contaminate the milk which may go sour or become spoiled sooner than if the vessels were tanninised. Domestic vessels not used for storing milk, such as water containers, are not frequently tanninised, although they may be treated periodically for colouration, quality improvement and preservation.

New utensils made of fibre or carved out of wood are usually treated with frankincense tannin. The process is, however, thought indispensable in the preparation of goatskin water containers that are commonly used in most areas in the frankincense region. The tanninisation method used is different from the smoking process for the milk vessels. The organic container is stuffed with pieces of frankincense bark dissolved in water which is allowed to remain inside the vessel for some days. Apart of the disinfecting and cleansing, this is done to make the container pure and free from organic stench. The method, which is applied periodically after the initial process, is also said to induce softness and elasticity.

The bark of the frankincense tree is not the only source of tannin. In areas outside the frankincense region other plants are variously exploited for the purpose. In the frankincense region, the fragrance of the bark of the frankincense tree offers superior quality in relation to other tannin-producing

---

[1] See chapter three on ownership.

plants. As a source of aromatic tannin, this fringe exploitation of the Boswellias contribute to their destruction.

The appearance of a tapped frankincense tree is likened, in one description, to that of a "decomposing animal". This is a fitting description considering the resin-exuding wounds scattered over the body of a tapped tree. Yet, more repulsive than this sight is that of a bare tree, its inside reddish resinous matter exposed by the removal of its bark for tannin. Unlike the customary grazing right over the foliage of the frankincense trees, cutting branches for browse or removing the bark for tannin without the approval of the "owners" is illegal. Nevertheless the removal of the bark of the trees by nomadic families without permission continues unabated.

Fumigation and purification

The mysterious appeal incense has had throughout human history and with which it is still connected in Somalia, seems to derive primarily from its ritual importance in divine worship. But already in ancient times people seem to have understood the more practical properties of the material. Groom mentions that in the eighth century B.C. the king of Egypt appointed men to purify the city of Memphis with natron and incense (Groom 1981:8). The first civilisations had considerable sanitation problems which could be met in most primitive ways. In the warm climates of the Mediterranean and the Middle East, putrefaction of waste sets in quickly and disagreeable smells pervaded the air. Pestilential insects, especially flies and mosquitoes, abounded and had to be kept away by a pleasant smoke. In such conditions incense and perfumes became necessary for comfortable living and were used widely. Frankincense and myrrh were among the most desirable materials used, not only for incense and perfumes but also for medicine. (*ibid.*:8)

Domestic fumigation is widespread among the Somalis who love perfumes in the same way their Muslim co-religionists the Egyptians still do. Better-off urban Somalis purify and incense their homes with a type of compounded incense known as *uunsi* which is processed and mainly traded by women. Despite the easy application of manufactured air fresheners, urban Somalis do not use them but prefer *uunsi* incensing. One can witness this custom in most Somali households in London. These keep various types of modern electric incense burners obtained from the Gulf states for the purpose. A Somali lady told me a story about her refugee girlfriend who was living in bed and breakfast accommodation in the Limehouse area in east London. One day she burned incense in her room. The fragrant smoke from the burned incense was sufficient to trigger the fire alarm.

Domestic fumigation is not restricted to urban areas but is much more widespread. Those who cannot afford the *uunsi*, like the urban poor, residents in rural villages and nomadic families, fumigate their homes with a ritual incense known as *foox* that is aromatic but not as fragrant as the *uunsi*. This is the lowest commercial grade of *beeyo* incense, the only locally traded quality. It consists of a mixture of bark flakes, powder or tiny pieces of incense. *Foox* is important both in terms of its widespread application and its use in ritual.

For purification purposes, *foox* incense is claimed to excel other types of local perfumes. In contrast to the pleasant smell created by the burning of the chiefly urban *uunsi*, *foox* incense is claimed to be both pleasant and able to dispel any bad smell. This sanitation benefit of *foox* incense is considered essential by most of the restaurants and stores in the larger towns and corresponding rural trading centres. Given inadequate or non-existent sanitation facilities, many restaurants and trading stores find it necessary to burn *foox* at least once a day, usually just before opening for business. To make a derelict apartment fit for habitation, the necessary treatment would not be complete without *foox* fumigation which purifies the aura of dereliction.

Fumigating or purifying the living place by burning incense has apparently a hygienic function, too. In practice this mundane function of the custom cannot be totally separated from the underlying religious dimension. Burning incense is customarily accompanied by seeking blessing from the Prophet and may be initiated by pronouncing "in the name of Allah the merciful the gracious", followed by the blessing of the family and its wealth or any other intent of immediate concern.

In addition to the custom of incensing their homes, Somalis fumigate some of the domestic vessels. Muller, noting the same custom in Sana, wrote: "In Sana moreover, the common custom has survived of turning jugs upside down over burning frankincense and of filling these jugs later on with water which takes on the taste of frankincense and is drunk while chewing qat" (Muller 1975:131). Somalis are inveterate *qat* chewers like the Yemenites, and fumigate water jugs for the same purpose. *Qat* was banned in Somalia in 1983 by the government, but is still illicitly chewed, particularly in the northern region. *Qat* is the stimulant leaves of the qat plant, <u>Catha edulis</u>. Some of the traditional water containers are also fumigated periodically in Somalia, to impart to the drinking water something of the pleasant aromatic and medicinal taste of the incense.

When guests are being entertained in the rural villages and nomadic hamlets of Somalia, it is essential to keep away the swarms of insects, flies and mosquitoes that thrive on the poor sanitation and torrid tropical heat. To drive away the insects while taking meals, incense is burned in the domestic incense burners.

Somalis do not use myrrh as fragrant incense for their country abounds with more aromatic products. Its smell is said to be offensive and suggestive of burning rubber. It is repulsive to snakes and is therefore burned to drive them away from nomadic huts.

Quoting past literature on the inhabitants of the Arabian Peninsula, Muller described a habit relating to hair and garment fumigation. Honour was shown to visitors by perfuming their garments on special occasions (cf. *ibid.*:131). Likewise, the urban Somalis and rich rural families apply manufactured perfumes to their guests as a mark of honour. At weddings and other public ceremonies, for example religious ceremonies, manufactured perfumes and ritual incense *foox* are liberally applied to participants. From a burning incense carried around the participants, each one in turn fans a share of the smoke towards his body. This habit has aims other than the practical body and garment incensing, too. It seems to be an act whereby participants partake of something of the purpose of the event.

Among the Somalis, at most social events, the practical clothing and bodily fumigation or perfume application, is often charged with religious intent, particularly the burning of ritual incense *foox*. One special type of hair fumigation is though apparently secular and widely practised by women, particularly those of the middle class families of northern Somalia. The ritual *foox* is not ideal for this, but the more fragrant *uunsi* incense. Balls of *uunsi* incense are burned in stone carved censers placed underneath the hair, so that the rising smoke passes through the shampooed and combed hair of the women.

At present, urban women apply strong perfumes and fumigate their hair for most casual events and some formal occasions, albeit that conventional Islamic behaviour allows women to do these things at home and for their husbands but not in public. Generally speaking, hair fumigation and the application of perfumes are considered as symbolic signs of seduction. If a married woman fumigates the apartment, incenses her hair and applies perfumes, this is considered by men an anticipation of romance.

In the foregoing discussion, I limited myself to the consideration of the two most common types of incense in Somalia, the chiefly ritual incense *foox* and the mainly urban *uunsi*. I did this partly because countless forms of aromatic products are used in different parts of Somalia, and partly because manufactured perfumes themselves are used for different specialised functions in different rites. These aspects of perfumes would require lengthy treatment beyond the scope of this volume.

Medicinal uses of frankincense and myrrh

Of the two types of frankincense produced in Somalia, *meydi* is not thought to have wider medicinal virtues. One informant told me that *meydi* resin is so powerful that it can tear a hole in a frankincense production uniform on the spot that it falls upon. This means that it is dangerous to apply to the body for treatment.

In the most westerly frankincense-producing area in Erigavo district, *beeyo* is used to treat venereal complaints and applied externally to wounds. A prepared solution of white pure tears of *beeyo* is drunk for these ailments and for back complaints. In some areas in Bosaso district, small drops of *beeyo* incense are swallowed to treat back ailments, too. In Alula district, a solution of incense taken as a drink is thought to treat a chronic cough, polio, and to relieve chest congestion.

The various medicinal virtues of the *beeyo* incense in different areas in the frankincense region of Somalia clearly demonstrate the elusive nature of the traditional medicine. Quite often the same prescription is variously applied to different ailments, thus defying any underlying systematic order, to the chagrin of the observer. Given this lack of consistency, one has to be careful about what treatment methods are used in a particular area, and the method of application, before reaching any general conclusions.

Most communities have their traditional doctors, who have admirable expertise in the indigenous medical lore. They are consulted for the treatment of illnesses that fail to respond to treatments based on commonplace medical knowledge possessed by most adult men. Sometimes if the treatment of the traditional healers fails to cure a particular sickness, an alternative local method may be tried, before the patient is finally taken to a modern hospital. This alternative venue is based on the scriptural medical texts kept by some of the learned men of religion. An elderly sheikh from Erigavo frankincense region told me the following medicinal virtues of *beeyo* incense, taken from a text titled *The book of compassion in medicine and wisdom*: "The white pristine drops of *beeyo* incense have a drying effect on the human body; they are useful in the treatment of acute coughs such as whooping cough; *beeyo* prevents or restricts an abnormal flow of organic fluids in the body; moreover, it improves intelligence and imparts valour."

Meydi incense produces inferior ritual incense *foox*, compared to the *beeyo* quality which yields better *foox* that is widely traded in Somalia. It is almost entirely produced for export to Saudi Arabia which consumes the bulk of the produce. In the frankincense region of Somalia, *meydi* is used as a chewing gum. It has a pleasant, perfumed and somewhat medicinal taste. Its chewing perfumes the breath. If chewed regularly, it is thought to protect the teeth from decay by cleansing them. Constant chewing is also thought to strengthen the gums.

Saudis seem to cherish the *meydi* chewing gum more than the Somalis, being willing to pay a high price for it. It appears so popular in Saudi Arabia that it has become an object of everyday domestic consumption. Somali traders report that Saudis attribute medicinal virtues to the product exceeding those reckoned by Somalis. As among the Somalis, chewing *meydi* is thought to protect the teeth and strengthen the gums, and its perfuming of the breath is a desired quality. Moreover, the Saudis are said to claim that *meydi* cleanses the alimentary canal and prevents stomach worm infestation. Apart from its medicinal attributes, Saudis seem to cherish the chewing *meydi* because it has become a prestigious social commodity consumed mostly by women in the household during social gatherings, and offered to honour guests.

Medicinal use of frankincense, in its turn, is of little importance in Somalia, compared to its fumigatory, purification and ritual function. Other plant products like myrrh are more useful than frankincense in local medicine. The present demand for myrrh mainly derives from its use in the manufacture of perfume and in incense sticks. It is also known to have a limited application in the preparation of mouth washes and gargles, in some special toothpastes, and some other pharmaceuticals.

Drake-Brockman noted that in modern times a diluted emulsion of myrrh is given to new-born children in Somaliland. It is also used for venereal ailments and in animal husbandry to increase the milk yield of female camels (1912:247). I am not certain whether myrrh in diluted emulsion form is given to infants in Somalia, but certainly myrrh is an ingredient of a protective charm worn around the neck of infants. The most important use of myrrh is thought to be its disinfectant ability. It is claimed to have a drying and healing effect on wounds, and therefore a plaster of thick myrrh emulsion is applied to the surface of a festering wound.

A thick emulsion of myrrh is daubed over the head of children suffering from infected skin diseases. The same is done for circumcised girls after the operation, to combat any possible infection of the mutilated reproductive organ. Afterwards, the application of myrrh on the wound is continued by making the girls sit over the smoke of myrrh burned inside a ground hole, to smoke the wound and disinfect it.

In many areas in northern Somalia throat infections, common cold and disturbances of speech, pain of the throat and glands are all treated with a drop of myrrh inserted underneath the delicate tissue of the tongue. Patients undergoing this treatment must bear the bitter taste of the gum (myrrh in Arabic is *murr* which means bitter and *malmal* in Somali).

Myrrh is also used to control men's sexuality. The sexual desire of adult men is thought to be reduced by drinking a solution of myrrh. Unmarried adult theology students are said to find this property quite useful to safeguard moral chastity and to be able to concentrate on their studies. More so in the past than in the present, young adult men suspected of overpowering sexual desire were recommended the treatment. But even at present, devout husbands separated from their wives and not approving of immoral sex, take a solution of myrrh to control their desire. I knew of a government official in Bosaso town using myrrh to save himself from adultery while his family was living in Hargeysa in the north. After prolonged use, the termination of the inhibitory impact of myrrh on the sex drive of men is locally referred to as "untying myrrh rope". To prepare a man for a normal sexual life, a fat ram is slaughtered and its meat cooked together with its fat. Eating this meat is thought to balance off the depressed sexual appetite brought about by the consumption of the myrrh solution. In northern Somalia, it is a joke to taunt the sexually weak by asking if they have been treated with myrrh.

The foregoing medicinal attributes of myrrh certainly do not exhaust all its local uses which are more widespread than the comparatively localised and limited medicinal uses of frankincense products. Myrrh is significant in the traditional medicine as an important disinfectant, while frankincense is important for sanitation as a fumigant and purifier.

Apart from the fact that it is used by adult Islamic students to suppress sexual drive, myrrh has other significant uses in the traditional Islamic learning institution. It forms a chief ingredient in preparing the ink used to write religious texts, hagiographies and historical works written by men of religion. The ink of the koranic schoolchildren in rural areas is made of myrrh dissolved with charcoal, sometimes with a small amount of sugar added. Writing with this local ink shines visibly on the student's wooden tablet.

Regarding the efficacy of the traditional medicine, successful cases concerning particular treatments are well remembered and widely disseminated to reinforce the traditional method. On the other hand, people tend to forget disastrous and unsuccessful cases, and perhaps unwittingly, to disregard the shortcomings of the tradition. Furthermore, determinism and fatalistic ideas are evoked to justify unsatisfactory results. For instance, in the event of no response to a treatment, it may be said that the time of the patient to recover has not yet come. It will come when Allah wishes so. It is this local tendency which remembers satisfactory treatment and conversely disregards glaring failures of traditional methods.

Ritual uses of incense burning

Ceremonies

Incense offering as a religious practice appears to have existed throughout human history, from the earliest civilisations to the present day. The significance of the tradition in the religious rites of peoples in the classical civilisations, the Sumerians and Babylonians, the Assyrians, the Hebrews, the Egyptians, the Persians and the Greeks are reviewed in Nigel Groom's study of 1981 (p. 21).

The Christian tradition initially rejected the practice, seeing it as a pagan rite, but later adopted it. In Islam, it does not constitute a prescribed part in a religious observance, yet it is widely used in the tradition, as a sacred perfume for the dead, and is offered in the shrines of the Muslim saints.

At present, offering incense in worship can be found in major traditions in the West as well as in the East, and it retains its universal appeal in religious practice. The sacred incense smoke rising upwards from a censer has a symbolic relationship to prayer, making the offering synonymous with worship (*ibid.*:2).

The sacramental attribute of ritual incense is frequently quoted in early literature. Frazer made an important distinction between perfumes for the Gods and perfumes used for sexual seduction, and explained that in ancient Arabia ritual observance was attached to the exploitation of frankincense trees which were thought to be sacred. Frankincense resin was considered holy, and the collectors were required to remain pure while gathering the resin. (Frazer 1957:106–7).

The hallowing of incense in ancient times due to its ritual importance, notwithstanding its practical applications, seems to have led to a great interest in the frankincense-producing lands. Muller (1975:132) remarked, "A country which produced expensive spices in abundance gave rise in antiquity to the idea of the legendary rich Sabeans living in luxury in the remote and happy frankincense region. The news about the country which brought forth plenty of frankincense by which one could obtain the favour of the Gods, went as far as China."

The frankincense region of Somaliland also assumed similar romantic feelings among early peoples. There is, however, no evidence to suggest that frankincense has earned Somalis substantial wealth comparable to that claimed to have been earned by early Arabians. Nevertheless, the frankincense trade has been important for their history and culture. Somaliland became known very early in history as a country blessed with various aromatic products and spices. Besides frankincense, it supplied other products unobtainable in the arid parts of southern Arabia. The ancient Egyptian's love for the country is epitomised by the celebrated names they gave to the region: "the land of punt", "the land of Gods", "the land of spices". The ancient Egyptian expedition to the legendary "land of Punt" undertaken during the reign of the powerful queen Hateshepsut in 1495 B.C. to fetch frankincense indicates the esteem they had for the fabulous incense region of Somalia.

Groom noted that demand for frankincense was very high during the Roman Empire and inflated its price. "Demand exceeded the supply, and transport expenses were high. Consequently the cost of frankincense and myrrh was considerable. By the time of the Roman Empire the enormous demand for these rare products had so swelled the price that they could be equated with gold. Thus we find gold, frankincense and myrrh together as the gifts brought to the infant Jesus in the legend of the Magi" (1981:8).

In general, ethnographic and theoretical data on ritual incense illustrate the paucity of information concerning this important religious subject. Therefore, I wish here to consider briefly some ethnographic examples of the custom in Somalia.

Somalis are almost exclusively Muslims who follow the orthodox Sunni Shaafi'ite Islamic Law. They share with south Arabians a penchant for perfumes in general: incense offering seems to be a residue of a pre-Islamic rite[2]. The Koran permits the use of *tib* in ordinary life, a generic word that encompasses many fragrant substances. However, incense offering does not

---

[2] For further information see Lewis 1969a.

constitute an essential part of the Muslim prayer but is widely used in the traditional rites.

Manufactured perfumes, which universally came into vogue after the 17th and 18th centuries, seem not to have eclipsed the importance of ritual incense in many ceremonies in Somalia; quite often they supplement each other in a particular rite. Except for specialised rites where the role of perfumes is indispensable, the traditional natural ritual incense, however, inspires an intense sacred sentiment not evoked to the same degree by the application of modern perfumes that are also widely used for secular purposes.

The availability of manufactured perfumes, incense sticks and a myriad of concocted incense compounds which have been integrated into most rituals in Somalia further complicates understanding the real purpose of the use. Multiple application of perfumes, as in many rituals, is most apparent in the *saar* ceremony. *Saar* spirits which afflict both men and women in southern Somalia and mainly women in the north (see Lewis 1969a:198–211), consume special types of perfumes. The existence of different *saar* spirits which belong to different transcendental groups are thought to be appeased by particular brands of perfumes. Women spirit priestesses identify the group of spirits that afflict the patient and recommend the specific type of perfume appealing to them. The correspondence between the ethnicity of afflicting spirits and the particularly favoured perfumes is necessary in the treatment. If the wrong perfume is offered to the spirits, they are claimed to get offended and take revenge by inflicting more harm to the patient.

The overriding importance of ritual incense in solemn rituals contrasts here with the overriding importance of particular brands of perfumes which are thought acceptable to different groups of spirits. The subordination of ritual incense to perfumes in the spirit possession cult in Somalia could be explained by the fact that *saar* is denounced by orthodox Islam as "pagan", and by men in northern Somalia as a foible of women engaging in "superstitious expensive exercises".

Broadly speaking, two types of possessing spirits are recognised, holy and unholy. Both spirits consume particular manufactured perfumes and certain types of food, and they differ in terms of their response to incense offering (see Lewis 1980:240–253). Ritual incense is thought appropriate to holy spirits: it is also offered to saints and used in other venerated Islamic ceremonies. Holy spirits have to be treated properly, and they are thought to respond positively to this sort of attitude. If they are offered perfumes and incense, and sumptuously feasted, they abandon the afflicted. Unholy spirits respond to their special perfumes but do not like ritual incense. They are forced out of the body of the afflicted by the burning of pungent substances. This testifies to the fact that ritual incense is associated with sacredness. It is offered to holy spirits and in the pursuit of good intentions. It is interesting to note that incense characteristically does not form part of the ingredients employed in malevolent magical rites with vocal intent to harm somebody or do something thought immoral. Tabooed objects like finger nails and human hair are objects usually used in witchcraft and other malevolent magical rites which, however, are very rare in northern Somalia.

Magical rites and the cult of saints

Like the *saar* ceremony, fortune-telling is chiefly a women's occupation, although most popular fortune-tellers are men rather than women. Fortune-tellers are often consulted by women who are considered by men as gullible beings squandering resources in un-Islamic rites. Only Allah is knowledgeable about future and forthcoming events, is the view of good Muslims. Indulgence in the practice is seen as intervention by ignorant human beings in the domain of Allah. In conspicuous disregard for the orthodox and eager to get an explanation for a misfortune or just to know more about the future, women and men consult fortune-tellers.

A female fortune teller *faaliso* is sometimes derogatively called *fooxiso*, the same way as a male fortune-teller *faaliye* is called *fooxiye*. The derogative names for male and female fortune-tellers literally mean "incense burner" and signify the importance of incense burning at the event. Some fortune-tellers undergo a traumatic transformation to carry out a prophecy. During the transformation they abandon their self and become possessed by prophecy spirits. They recite magical spells while frankincense is liberally burned in the domestic censer.

The role of incense in prophecy is most important in the actual future speculation for the consultant or identification of the cause of a particular misfortune. For instance, to identify the cause of an illness, infertility, or continual loss of children, the fortune-teller burns incense on the censer placed in front of him. The crux of the rite is a fixed gaze by the operator on the ascending fumes. Reading the ascending smoke from the pattern it makes, the fortune-teller eventually reveals the explanation which is translated into plain language for the consultant.

What we see in the prophecy rite, is the importance given to the burning of the ritual incense which is here imbued with magical quality by projecting it as the mirror image through which explanations for occurrences are revealed. The custom is absolutely crucial for the performance, just as manufactured perfume is essential in appeasing spirits in the *saar* ceremony. The function incense offering has in these magical contexts is remarkably distinct from the holiness it assumes in the traditional Islamic rites, i.e. reciting Koran and reading the Prophet Mohammed's birthday service in Islamic calendars.

It is thought that two times a day, early morning and evening, are particularly propitious for incense burning, although domestic fumigation for purification or practical fumigation could be carried out at any time. This fumigation is held to shield the dwelling from malicious spirits who are in an eternal struggle with good Muslims and bent on dissuading them from the Islamic way of living. In addition to the protective role, this custom has another important supplementary function, that of attracting holy spirits, the guardians of faithful Muslims. These two antagonistic spirits never reside together in the same place at the same time. The holy spirits dispossess and drive away the evil ones once they are invited through observance of Islamic faith.

As a matter of fact, in everyday family concerns that do not necessarily call for the conduct of a large blessing ceremony *duco*, it is usually the burning of incense that acts as a means of propitiating the assistance of Allah or the ancestral saints in attending to the immediate concerns of the family. If a segment of the herd goes astray, the prayer for the protection of the animals from marauding beasts is solemnly recited at the evening incensing. Apart from warding off evil spirits from home and inviting holy spirits, incensing in the ritual sense represents an easy and quick form of propitiation for the family.

In lieu of direct communication with the ultimate source of grace, Allah, Somalis commonly refer to a hierarchy of saints, to intercede with the prophet on their behalf. To make merit for the saints, most of whom are clan ancestors, and to assert that they are remembered by their descendants are some of the important aims in the veneration of saints (cf. Lewis 1980:248–251).

The veneration of saints takes the form of organised large-scale periodic visitations to their tombs. Feasting, reciting the Koran and the Prophet Mohammed's birthday service, are noteworthy in the commemoration of saints. Reciting of the holy text and the tradition is supplemented by burning incense, which is offered throughout the course of the event.

In the tombs of the great saints, presents of manufactured perfumes which may be explained like the *saar* ceremony in terms of their un-Islamic origin accumulate over time. These are offered to saints by the visitors. Many shrines contain receptacles for incense offering. At graves without such receptacles, one can often find earthen or stone carved censers for the purpose. Unlike its function in magical rites such as the prophecy one, the tradition in the context of saint veneration assumes sacred overtones. I do not think it may be thought of as food for the saints or as an independent form of worship. It may be described as contrite behaviour aimed at winning the favour of the saints, to induce them to intervene effectively on behalf of Muslim followers. It seems to function as a means of promoting the pursuit of the purpose in hand, by creating currents of religious feeling during the performance.

Alfred Gell's (1977) hypothesis on the smell sign seems to apply to the role of ritual incense. He explained the profound connection between the smell aspect and other worldliness. He showed that a Umeda villager's outlook intimately connects smelling with dreaming, which represents access to higher truth. The smell sign is explained as an ideal model of exchange between different domains—this world and the transcendental. In this context, the sacred fragrant smoke of the ritual incense gives access to higher truth without leaving the realm of things that are intelligible.

CHAPTER SIX

Frankincense sector poetry

Pastoral metaphors

In the preceding chapter on property, we saw the influence of pastoral concepts on the classification of property among northern Somalis. Wealth is categorised into pastoral or animate and non-pastoral or inanimate. In this chapter, we will witness the same tenacity of the pastoral culture and its influence on non-pastoral groups in northern Somalia, using a cultural idiom, that of oral poetry.

The elaborate types and styles of poetry and the tremendously deep and profuse literary heritage, has led to the Somalis being characterised as "a nation of bards". Some aspects of the social dimension of the poetic craft have been incisively documented by students of Somali language and culture. Unlike their western counterparts, Somali poets are not a professional cadre who communicate with a sophisticated but a limited elite group in the midst of an indifferent mass population. On the contrary, they are ordinary people who on their own initiative have mastered the skill of the craft and therefore effectively communicate with an enthusiastic wider society through the medium. Somali poets come from all walks of life and do not necessarily originate from a particular social or economic stratum.

Although an impressive style and high linguistic standard are admirable qualities of a successful poem, nevertheless it is the "social connotation" that is often most appreciated by both critics and wider audiences. Andrzejewski and Lewis (1964:2) cogently expressed the point: "It is designed to influence the opinion either of a body of kinsmen or of the public at large. Thus some of the serious poems incite kinsmen to avenge past wrongs. Others foment them, and praise and blame are most effectively spread throughout the country through this medium. For example verse spreads most rapidly and is not easily forgotten, serious poetry indeed is closely allied to oratory, another art which Somalis esteem and in which they excel."

Apart from the crucial role poetry plays in clan politics, a topic which is adequately documented in the Somali context, another important function has also been noted by Somali ethnographers. The authors cited in the foregoing paragraph wrote: "Oral poetry assumes a pervasive importance and appeal because it does the role of broadcasting information as effectively as the press and radio in a country where although a few can read, news travel with amazing rapidity" (ibid.:2). These factors and the appreciation by the Somalis for the poetic language in lieu of prose, explain the significance of the oral craft.

Samatar (1982) approached the subject from a particular perspective by examining the relation between oral poetry and politics in Somalia. He ably discussed an example of the effective harnessing of the art by a charismatic national leader in the colonial resistance movement. A relatively puritanical messiah preaching the new Salahiya Islamic order, no less than the astute political leader, Sayid Maxamad Cabdalla Xasan, employed the medium in which he excelled in order to organise the dervish army against colonial infidels for a period of two decades.

My approach to poetry could be considered distinct in the sense that it represents a micro-level economic analysis of Somali poetry. Despite the fact that frankincense sector Somali poems portray a distinct and localised culture in relation to the pastoral and other sedentary cultures, they are impressively replete with metaphors and imagery derived from the overarching nomadic way of life.

I gathered verses during my fieldwork, and most of them are short praise and work songs. Some of them do also have the qualities of the more serious and elaborate versification that addresses pastoral, philosophical and historical issues. Praise and work songs are chanted while collecting incense, and in Erigavo district where the traditional *dhaanto* dance is very popular, some of the work and praise songs are chanted by incense collectors for the dance.

The first section of the chapter shows how antagonism between different economic groups is expressed through poetic discourse. A dominant theme is the comparison and denigration of one or the other group and illustrates this tendency. Most importantly, it shows the way the superordinate pastoral culture imposes itself on non-pastoral groups in the context of oratory. Traditional stock breeding undoubtedly moulds the world view of the Somalis in general, and enormously influences the fabric of their social world. Frankincense collectors not unlike others derive metaphors and images from the overarching pastoral system, in the versification of their exploits. The following dialectics of a discourse between commercial frankincense forests and camel herds elucidate the point.

The first verse, from Galgala village, Bosaso district, elaborates some important features of the frankincense economy.

> It (frankincense forests) does not require transhumance into the interior of Nugaal
> Nor does it pasture on grass and it refrains from water altogether
> It is not persistently moved after the fresh grass of the latest rain
> The sites at the mountain caverns of Lumanka, and the glens of Indhacad andHoohaale
> Our Boswellia forests never fail to yield some reserve resin (milk)
> Which is continually milked out for economic exploitation
> Nothing else except the "red guinea"[1] could buy the incense commodity
> May Allah not deprive me of the frankincense forests for they are my herds. (11)

The poet spokesman for the frankincense people makes a comparison between their mode of livelihood and that of the pastoral economy. The limitations of the latter are laboured to mark the superiority of the former. Frankincense forests do not browse, nor do they depend upon drinking water, a scarce resource that is responsible for the constant and rather erratic movement of pastoralists. To distinguish the semi-settled pattern of frankincense collectors from the transhumance of pastoralists, frankincense property is described as fixed property.

The poet glorifies the frankincense economy which is claimed to be free from pastoral impediments. However, it is interesting to note that in the concluding

---

[1] The red guinea is the old Somali name for the British gold coin worth nominally £ 1.00, but in poetic language symbolising money in general.

line of verse, commercial forests are described as being as important as herds. Thus the trees are milked of resin in the same way animals are milked by the nomads. The resin produced from the incense trees sustains life by earning the cultivator income which is purchased with staple food, just as animals and their products support the nomadic populace. In short, if livestock does not fail the herder, commercial forests do not fail the frankincense gatherer. The assertion that only money can buy frankincense merchandise attests a long-standing commercial culture of the crop which collectors point out to excel in relation to other local economies.

Despite the glorification of frankincense in the text, and the denigration of pastoral herds, the major objective of subordinating herds to frankincense is, I think, undermined by the poet's allusion to his trade as animal wealth in the concluding line. For want of a better term to express the importance of frankincense, the poet describes it as being as important as herds.

The analogy obtaining between the frankincense crop and camels is better expressed in this song which has been obtained from Galgala village.

> May I identify our camels
> They are resin impregnated grey ones
> that grow on the mountain range
> And bear tapping incision marks on their bark. (12)

The song points out some important features of the frankincense industry. To present familiarisation in a popular idiom, frankincense is designated as camels. Not to allow the analogy to obscure the crucial difference between the rival systems, frankincense forests are characterised as resin impregnated compared to milk impregnated camels. In contrast to the mobile herds which move seasonally from one region of pasturage to another, frankincense grows and thrives in the maritime frankincense region.

The tapping wounds that are administered on the bark of the frankincense trees, are figuratively described as marks in the last line of the song. The act of marking, more than the significance it may have for the description of the trees, seems to represent an element of control. Pastoral herds bear brands which denote ownership. Similarly, the tappings along the bark of frankincense trees mark control rights of the tapper over the incense crop. In an almost identical song in Erigavo district, the tapping instrument *mingaaf* is described as literally watching over the frankincense trees. What is implied is not vigilance in the same way that pastoralists keep vigil over herds; rather, the metaphor tends to emphasise a unique system of resource exploitation where frankincense trees are tapped with a knife to procure commercial resin.

In the search for advantage over the rival economic systems, frankincense collectors are quick to raise the market orientation of the incense crop. The first verse has already pointed out the fact, but I would like to consider some more examples of songs which show frankincense as an export item of trade. The songs were obtained in Erigavo district.

> A garment wears out in time
> And wealth may vanish
> We own permanent port facility
> And export *meydi* incense. (13)

The song claims other types of wealth are not permanent. As stated in the preceding chapter, urban property of money and buildings may be lost any time. And drought may decimate nomadic herds. Resistant to drought and more endurable than urban property are permanent natural port facilities and the incense crop obtained from drought-resistant frankincense species.

Many songs articulate tangible benefits of frankincense exploitation for the producers. Here are a few examples:

Despised incense *beeyo*
during the harsh *xagaa* season
It is wealth
That can buy clothes. (14)

When the hot season of *xagaa* commences
And the *gu'* rains of plenty recede
And other peoples are starving to death
Is the best time for *beeyo* producers. (15)

As clearly expressed in the songs gathered in Erigavo district, frankincense families are said to enjoy an advantage, that is access to imported goods, i.e. clothes and food made possible by exported incense. This advantage is indeed not limited to them in modern times because of the large-scale commercialisation of livestock which are exported from the natural coastal harbours in the frankincense region in the same way as frankincense.

Ignoring the weakness of the frankincense economy, the songs preach about pastoral families starving to death during the critical dry season *xagaa*. This is the season of prosperity and harvest for incense collectors. To try to convince women that incense men are better men (young men from different economic groups compete for women by praising their exploits), it is argued that they could afford to buy gifts of clothes and provide imported food for them at times of privation for the pastoral people.

The analogy between the frankincense economy and the superordinate pastoral system is much wider. In the domestic sphere , an elderly incense man resuming frankincense collection after a period in which he engaged in herding, had this to say concerning a missed staple diet or bread baked inside the ashes of a fire. In a rather nostalgic tone, he described the diet of bread as more invigorating than the fresh milk of a camel soon after giving birth. The verse is from Galgala village.

If it is (bread) warm and sparkling
With sticking ashes and embers flying off its surface
It is more invigorating than the fresh milk of a recently calved camel
If you could serve it to me in just a moment. (16)

Short praise and work songs of this type show the preponderance of the camel culture that influences heavily the outlook of the frankincense collectors. Such predisposition is general and, as will be seen shortly, is also true of the sedentary cultivators in the northwest. It is evidence of the degree to which the cultural pattern of non-pastoral communities are permeated by pastoral values.

The competition for excellence between different economic groups is quite often between the dominant pastoral system and some other subsistence form. However, the battle is sometimes carried out between sedentary groups in the northern region. In the verse below, frankincense collectors in Erigavo district portray their trade as all-important in relation to pastoralism and crop production. Incense men sing this song in folklore dances to persuade women to join them.

Trading agricultural goods is denigrated as petty local business and therefore the province of small-scale women traders, while frankincense is an export good which is traded through large enterprise like the National Trading Agency, shortened in Italian to E.N.C. Tipping the balance beforehand in order to cajole the opinion of women folk, the singer finally asks, which men would they like to go with, frankincense men or cultivating men.

> The men who produce long tears of resin
> The best quality *mushaad* and gleaned inferior grades
> Finally settle accounts with E.N.C.
> And the men who deal and have ties with urban women traders
> where their meagre agricultural surplus
> Is hauled aboard a trade truck
> For trading in the distant capital city, Xamar
> You girls with the smart look of silk
> In the name of justice
> Which men would you like to go with? (17)

The sector glorification verses examined so far articulate a theme of economic value. Two types of representations that coexist but are analytically contradictory are expressed. Carried away by innocuous and snobbish banter, it is thought appropriate to equate commercial forests with cherished camel herds. In a different representation camels are subordinated to the frankincense property. In the context of sector glorification the underlying contradictions may not be apparent to the poet. His aim is to ennoble the fundamental community resource base. If at times, he presents frankincense to be as important as camels for better description, instead of sustaining the superiority of his trade, he is doing so unwittingly, within the constraints of the pastoral culture that permeates the outlook of most Somalis.

Sector constraints and antagonism expressed in poetry

The cultural idiom of oral poetry which frankincense people employ to glorify their economic base is also used to express the constraints and endemic problems of their sector. The following verses substantiate a pragmatic consideration of the plight of the incense collectors.

Aware of the perpetual debt that haunts many incense collectors, a new initiate prophesied:

> Either I manage to settle my debt this season
> And accumulate some surplus
> For the benefit of purchasing camels from Dalawa market
> Or fall into debt
> And never again cultivate *beeyo* incense. (18)

A few more examples gathered from Galgala village will further indicate the sector constraints, bitterly versified by incense poets.

A man early in the morning set out for work
Taking off his usual dress, donned the filthy work clothes
In the evening about half a measure of cereals
Helped himself to his mouth
Let alone fitness and health
I fear of death and corpses picked up by vultures. (19)

"Abandon herding your stock"
"Never take refuge under the shade of a tree"
Is the lot of frankincense producer
May Allah save us from such a misery
"Mr. 'X' has not shown for work in this cycle"
"But I was committed and braced myself for work"
Is the lot of frankincense producer
May Allah save us from such misery. (20)

Several sector constraints are pointed out in the verses, in addition to the previously mentioned perpetual indebtedness of the producers. The intensive work of resin collection in a difficult environment; meagre diet of dry bread which lacks animal products, milk, purified ghee and meat that are thought most nourishing; and conflicts between the joint unit of frankincense production in relation to work ethic.

The artistic praise language which glorifies the frankincense industry is here replaced with lamenting verses denouncing the occupation as daunting, less remunerative and ultimately miserable. This ambivalent attitude towards the primary resource of the community, could be considered a general tendency notable among northern Somalis regardless of economic specialisation.

Similarly, peasants in the northwest region glorify and speak openly about the adversity of sedentary life. Gardening is viewed as a difficult task in relation to animal husbandry in average years. They say there is always some work to be done in the field. First of all the land has to be prepared for planting. Then the planted crop has to be tended. Choking weeds have to be cleared away. And all the time crops have to be protected from domestic animals. At the ripening stage swarms of hungry birds have to be pelted away all day long. In some areas, during the nights men watch for wild pigs that can devastate the crop.

The demanding farming tasks are supported by a belief which reckons farming as a punishment imposed upon sedentary human beings in general. The ancestors of human society, Adam and Eve, were originally living in heaven. Their eternal enemy (Satan) tried to corrupt them by persuading them to eat a forbidden fruit growing in heaven. Eventually he succeeded in corrupting Eve, as a consequence of which they were thrown out of heaven into the natural world. From the bounty in heaven where everything that is desired was available without effort, the ancestors had no alternative other than to support themselves. They started to practise agriculture which is thought to have been imposed as punishment for this original sin. The myth could be interpreted in various ways. It could be argued that it reveals the moral superiority of men over women. It was Eve not Adam that was corrupted. Indeed Somalis hold that women are morally more susceptible than men who are viewed as moral guardians. I am not certain whether the myth has such agricultural connotations in other Muslim countries, but certainly in the north of Somalia it is used to rationalise agricultural work and its origin.

But having the "God-given" constraints, sedentary communities in the agricultural northwest possess an elaborate body of verses and work songs. Like frankincense collectors they glorify and subordinate camels to farming through the poetic discourse in which the contest for honour between different economic groups is conducted.

The focus of many of their work songs is the plough-oxen which are the companions of the cultivator in the gardening season. The frequent analogy drawn between camel herds and farming by agriculturalists, for whom cattle replace camels as the primary stock, shows the influence of the pastoral world view on these recently sedentarised groups.

The following songs are taken from an unpublished source at the Somali Academy of Sciences and Arts in Mogadishu. They were collected by a research worker, Cabdi Cabdillaahi Ducaale (1984), who was based in the Academy office in Hargeysa. The English translation is mine.

To brace the plough-oxen for the task, the farmer sings:

I have relinquished pleasure
And never enjoy the fresh milk of recently calved camels
And you (oxen) must also abandon the delight of Madar pasture
and all other good things. (21)

While tilling the land, if he detects signs of fatigue or clumsiness from the oxen, the farmer admonishes:

Like terrified and fleeing camels
That long wandered astray in the wilderness
My white streaked *Caare* (name of an ox)
You lost your swift move. (22)

The sluggish movement of the draft animal is likened to that of desperate camels which have lost their energy as a result of persistent danger in the wilderness. In the former song, to console the work-oxen, the farmer tries to convince them that he himself made a sacrifice to do gruelling farm labour. He relinquished the enjoyment of fresh camel milk. It seems unusual for a farmer practising crop production and supplementary cattle breeding to retort that he relinquished regaling himself with camel milk. Most appropriately he should have rued that he missed cattle milk and sorghum diet.

To glorify their system, not unlike frankincense producers, cultivators in one instance exalt their crops to the rank of camels. In another instance they elevate them above all other rival occupations. These divergent representations of economic comparison at times unwittingly coexist in the same verse. Here are some more examples of poetic analogies between agriculture and other economic forms.

If the planting season *shinni* commences
At the onset of the short season *shinni gaabey*
I may exchange for you the long-legged pony
And an ideal woman partner
Certainly not for five milch camels. (23)

At the beginning of the farming season, when investment in land overrides all other considerations, the plough-oxen are the most valuable property. The cultivator would not surrender them for any price, not even for five milk camels. However, he may be seduced to exchange them for a suitable wife, and a strong horse, as northern Somalis traditionally value horses more than the other domestic species. These goods coveted by the cultivator are the ones a nomad may also exchange for his beloved camels.

We have observed earlier that pastoralism as the superordinate culture is constantly used as a standard for economic excellence by non-pastoral poets. At those euphoric moments of sector glorification, venerated pastoralism is subordinated to the economy concerned. The following songs express the advantage crop production is claimed to have over stock breeding.

> Those who inhabit the Qaaliga pastoral region
> And milk camels is the Qadowga country
> Are despising us
> But would ultimately beg us favours. (24)

The purchase of sorghum from the sedentary cultivators, which is most pronounced in the dry season when milk yield from pastoral herds is greatly reduced, is considered as a mark superiority of farmers. It is implied that the pastoral system which derides farming is fundamentally not self-sufficient as it advocates, and ultimately depends upon crops produced by their arch rivals.

The benefits of agricultural specialisation are noted after a bumper crop. The status it confers by attracting others is well brought out in the following songs. The present songs are chanted by the flailing parties thrashing the harvested sorghum. Many of these songs and others show the Oromo influence which is linked to historical introduction of cultivation in this style from Harar region in Ethiopia (cf. Lewis 1961a:102).

> When the critical time starts to grip
> And the milk yield of livestock diminishes
> *Alla kaniyow in aabe*—sorghum crop
> Brings all people to our door
> Hoo hoo hoo. (25)

> Someone who fails to get a supply of sorghum
> Either desperately sells his calf
> Or abandons his own son
> Hoo hoo hoo. (26)

> My God, someone who harvest a bumper crop
> *Badda nageeye*—sorghum
> Can afford to do whatever pleases him
> Hoo hoo hoo. (27)

I realise that the Somali expressions which refer to the sorghum crop need an explanation, but truly I do not know their etymology, and their direct translation does not render a clear meaning. For instance *badda nageeya* is literally translated as "pacifier of the ocean", which may signify that sorghum as a staple crop smoothens the life of the sedentary people. With an adequate supply a man is said to enjoy a good life; lack of it could cause the farmer to resort to all sorts of aberrant behaviour, like fleeing from his dependent family, or desperately selling young cows that will increase the herd.

In contrast to the analogy often drawn between cultivation and nomadic herds, the present songs explain the legitimate exploitation of the plough-oxen, and at least articulate a distinct feature of the sedentary life. The subsistence sorghum crop is cogently expressed as wealth (plant wealth) which is buried underneath the ground waiting to be procured by the cultivator with the support of the plough-oxen.

To get effective service from them, farmers sometimes go beyond persuasion and remind the draft animals of their obligations.

I would have pampered you
And never have rigorously exploited you
But my kids are crying for support
And I seek subsistence from the land. (28)

You are not a slim necked girl
To be expected from marriage
Nor are you a young calf
To be expected of progeny
There is wealth buried underneath the ground waiting for our joint exploitation. (29)

The sector oratory examined so far reveals that non-pastoral groups in the northern region of Somalia, for want of a better analogy utilise metaphors and concepts of pastoral provenance. This predisposition itself is sufficient indication of the extent to which the nomadic life permeates the thought of the society regardless of economic specialisation. We have seen frankincense forests symbolised as being as economically important as herds. In other words here, as in the currency compensation transactions between lineages (in cares of physical injury of a person or homicide) where a certain amount of cash that is less than the actual value of the compensation in camel units changes hands, people are operating on a camel standard.

Another aspect of this oratory is that the battle for excellence between rival economic groups, necessarily requires the glorification of the economic system concerned in relation to others. The merits of particular subsistence economy are rather exaggerated. Its institutional constraints are diplomatically concealed to project a flawless industry transcending others in which their shortcomings are expanded upon.

This contextually-based economic representation, concerning the primary resource base of different economic groups, is uniquely amended with a pragmatic view. Poet spokesmen of sedentary cultivators and frankincense collectors not only sing the praises of their respective economies, they also express through the same media, the constraints and limitations of their trade. The chief economic activity is amusingly denounced as a miserable and necessary evil, a tendency which is equally true of the pastoralists.

Underlying the competition between rival economic systems indicated in the foregoing discussion, seems to be some sort of sector antagonism and competition for land and water resources. Verbal antagonism does not entirely coincide with the social distribution and organisation of the rival economic groups, despite the fact that certain clans, and particular lineages within clans may dominate the practise of a particular mode of production. Thus it is not uncommon that a considerable proportion of cultivating lineage members still practise mobile pastoralism, and equally that some members of frankincense gathering lineages engage in nomadism. Presumably antagonism between economic groups is most intense when lineage ties and economic specialisation coincide.

Most commonly some sort of antagonism obtains between contiguous systems, such as pastoralism and cultivation or pastoralism versus frankincense production. At the highest level there seems to be an opposition between the dominant superordinate pastoral culture and relatively localised sedentary systems. Sedentary cultivators and frankincense collectors, because of their unreflective or uncritical dependence upon pastoral concepts and metaphors in their endeavour to glorify their trades, illustrate the fact that they could be considered as localised activities struggling for survival and identity in the framework of a dominant pastoral world.

Frankincense theft curse

The verses below explain the past theft of frankincense, a practice that prevailed with intensity before the 1969 revolution. Theft was carried out by organised banditry and was not limited to frankincense communities but also terrorised rural communities in general. Animal theft was as common as frankincense stealing. Storing harvested frankincense in open mountain caves as well as the fact that collectors abandoned incense collection sites at the intervals between the harvest cycles to return to the nomadic hamlet, made incense most vulnerable to pilfering and plunder.

Some isolated cases of theft were reported in some places during my field work, particularly in some areas in Erigavo region. Where the problem exists, a guard is contracted to keep vigil over the collected merchandise at the height of the harvest, although in general the practice is becoming a thing of the past. Thus the cited poems refer to the period before the present regime.

An incense collector in a village in Bosaso district became suspicious about a local thief, anticipating that he would steal his frankincense. Without naming him, as the etiquette requires, he denigrated the villain in three lines.

Deceptively dressed like a moustached gentleman, but with a woman's honour
If he sneaks into every cache to know all the secrets
He is treacherously waving hernia-distended testicles for
an incense cave-store to plunder. (30)

The suspected thief is represented as one with woman's virtue. Honour which Somalis greatly value, is primarily conferred by one's lineage, although it can be buttressed by individual qualities like courage, hospitality and skill in oratory. Honour is a man's prerogative in male-dominated Somali society. To label a man as possessing woman's attributes is one of the worst forms of abuse. What gives efficacy and power to the substance of the abuse is the art in which it is expressed. That which is couched in poetic language is thought to carry more weight than plain language.

The damage to honour that invective poem can cause is long-standing and in acute cases considered more damaging than physical assault. It is here that the function of the verse lies. The poet seems to have warned the local thief by composing the abusive verse—a pretext to dissuade him not to steal his property. The most potent verses of the Somali poetic repertoire are "curse poems". They are commonly composed by the aggrieved to direct deserved punishment upon the guilty who may or may not be known. A typical verse is that of a sheikh in Gudmo-biyo-cas village in Erigavo district. Hassan was robbed of work uniforms he bought for his labouring sons the other day.

> They confided the sad news as I prepared the ablution
> The performed prayer and expiation had been spoiled by distraction
> the *fatiha* chapter has not been validly recited
> The meticulously organised tools and equipment provided for the boys
> Were taken away yesterday by those whom Allah may dismember their organs
> If my property is not retrieved, I am an elder parent
> What I pronounce has caused many deaths in the past
> And now I want to call Allah, the Almighty guardian
> May the theft of the immaculate pieces of cloth cause your death
> Forever, from one generation to the next experience persistent bereavement
> Lose your fertility and your testicles get transformed into skin water drawing vessel *wadaan*
> Your descendants get condemned to everlasting grief
> I wish to dig your grave unceremoniously with simple branches of *xogor* and *haam* trees
> Do your funeral service with a broken fence-making stick *hangool*
> The perdition cry be the eternal call that echoes from your quarter
> As long as you live, wear the "mourning scarf" of bitterness. (31)

Samatar (1982:80) has classified the various forms of curse used by Somalis according to their function and source (see Table 4). In practice, these types overlap and may not be as distinct as the typology suggests. For instance, the curser could be both a parent, religious man and poet. The type of curse which such a person uses would depend upon the context. As a parent he may pronounce *habaar* towards his unruly child, and as a poet he can pronounce *kuhaan* against a rival clan on behalf of his group.

Table 4. *Types of Somali curse*

TYPE	USABLE BY	OBJECT
Inkaar	All living things, including plants and animals. This type of curse is a weapon for the weak against the predatory plundering of the powerful.	The powerful, the oppressor and those who use their advantage over others to irresponsible ends.
Na'lad	God Prophets Angels	Sinners, non-believers, liars, troublemakers in the community of faith.
Habaar	Intelligent beings: men, angels, parents and elders.	Infidels, disobedient children, oppressors.
Asmo	*Wadaads*: Men of God	Rival clans
Yu'asho, Kuahaan (also known as *guhaan* or *haafil*)	Poets	Blatant offenders, rival clans.

The way the poet's pronounced curse is thought to possess efficacy to achieve the stated misfortune or punishment, has been ably explained by the same author. He wrote, "This is the poet's curse and rests on the belief among

Somalis that the poet has, as it were, 'a hotline' to the Deity and can therefore intervene, through his poetic oration, in natural events. The compound of poetic verse *Kuhan* is called *afkuleeble*, 'he whose mouth is a dart'. An *afkuleeble* is at once weird, clairvoyant and prophetic: he is believed to foretell the future, to possess omniscient attributes and to perceive things beyond the natural range of mortal men. His malevolent orations are compared to lethal arrows which fly across the Somali desert and come home to the hearts of those who incur his displeasure, causing joy among his friends and consternation among his enemies" (*ibid.*:81).

Samatar also explained the maintenance of the belief in the efficacy of poetic curses and how these assume such attributes. Somalis apparently chose to remember events and circumstances in which a poetic curse has somehow proved efficacious, while forgetting those situations in which poetic curse proved ineffective (*ibid.*:82).

The poet in the example has the qualities which could qualify him as a potential curse source. He is an elder, and claims that his poetic words are potentially lethal, speaking from past experience. Given the elder's status and his religious inclination, as well as the general belief about the power of the poetic curse, I was not surprised to hear from my informants that the bandits died in mysterious circumstances soon after the composition of the curse. Relevant events, in our example the death of the thieves sometime after the performance, are explained as the consequence.

Items used in the production of frankincense such as the work uniform, cooking utensils, the tapping instrument and grinding stone, were all subject to frequent stealing in the past. The most serious of all was the theft of incense merchandise. A man who abandoned his nomadic homestead in a distant pastoral territory to cultivate frankincense expressed his concern of a possible theft of his labour.

> The cultivation of frankincense that has sapped my strength during the preceding
> *xagaa* season
> And made me forget the guardianship role of my family and others
> My God, he who steals it, may never enclose lawfully acquired property in a *kraal*. (32)

The poet wishes any one who steals the fruit of his labour which cost him dearly, e.g. temporary abandonment of his family, to subsist forever on filth and forbidden bread. The consequence of this in the afterlife is God's wrath and eternal hell.

As to why incense theft remarkably diminished in the revolutionary period, many informants claim that people had become "civilised" and had grown out of such illicit and morally wrong practices. Nowadays, it is said, people prefer to work and earn a living in an honourable way instead of by plunder. However, the crucial factor which may have greatly curtailed the practice and, to a considerable extent, restored peace and order in both rural and urban areas is a heavy-handed clamp down by the government on crime.

A poetic contest about an imagined prostitute

Frankincense collectors in Bosaso district have a possibly unique poetic contest which centres on an imaginary invisible woman. The principal rule of the contest is that she must continually move between work parties residing in collection sites in a particular area. She is formally deployed in a particular site by a composed poem which conveys her over the physical terrain from departing site to a new destination. The receiving party pass her to another site in return.

To avoid a possible disruption of her movements, she is not usually sent to a site whose occupants are known not to excel in poetry. At least one tenant of the joint production unit must be competent in the craft to participate in the game.

Frankincense collectors in Bosaso district who entertain this transhumant woman do not credit themselves with having originated this style of poetic contest. They admit that they borrowed it from townspeople who similarly passed her between towns and villages across the frankincense region.

Why is she denied residence or sojourn in any place for a time? Because she is portrayed as amoral, with inverted attributes to those of an ordinary woman. In poetry she is described as a prostitute and sometimes as a stupid donkey.

Being a prostitute or loose woman, she is never welcome in any place. Wherever she lands, however temporarily, she brings shame. Therefore in haste she is passed on to another rival quarter.

The following long poem, was composed by a 17-year-old high school student studying in Bosaso town. At the time he was cultivating incense with his three brothers near Galgala village where his parents live. After receiving the amoral woman from another site, Geedi conveyed her from the residing site, Jeeni-dheere about an hour's walk to the north of the village, through the village and from there on to Booj site which is roughly two hours walk west of the village. In the journey, we will see how the young poet articulately maps out the route the woman had to take towards her new destination. Sometimes she had to run, at other times she had to scurry or tread carefully over the rugged terrain. The poem was composed on June 12, 1985.

> Bracing ourselves for work at early hours of the day break
> We set out for Boydo, the site of *beeyo* frankincense species
> As soon as we got here, we met Beyluul (woman) in the middle of the site
> Geedi went for her and asked the news
> She reported that there is prosperity and peace
> Although she had been evicted by a group who directed her up the mountain
> They advised not to miss there, what is described as the abode of nice boys
> Whatever, I am desperate and in need of food
> Geedi made a fire and instantly cooked a kilo of pasta
> Put on the kettle and served her a quick tea
> After taking her fill, with satisfaction
> She said, you work incense and are ready to go for work
> Tell me the site I want to go there
> I said let me tell the news, my sister Bilan
> If I got hundreds of sheep that graze in the mountain
> Or habitually bred the grey cattle herds in the country
> Or owned camel stock available to be milked with the left hand
> Or migrated to the Arabian peninsula to earn money
> If I were a driver of trade truck *Sabaax* or a military truck

If I got substantial money deposited in the world banks
Or else if I am a professional incense collector residing at Booj site
Bilan, I would never send you away, for lies must not be told
I am a poor student who does not have hundreds
If God wills and we are protected from misfortune
As soon as this month finishes, we all have to go
Dear sister, we will go to Bosaso for study
Let me elaborate the physical terrain of your trip
The track will take through the uprising that is abundant with *moxor* trees
Continue moving forward, I wish you safe through the barren cliff track
Then you will descend to the valley and uneven lowland
Pass on to clamber up the opposite ascending slope
It will lead to the even surface with the bulky *dhamas* trees
Mind this is the grave yard of a revered sheikh who is never passed
Quickly offer him the prayer, he deserves more than this
Take the left one of the bifurcating track
There is land abundant with date palm ahead of you
Its panorama shines from the distance when you arrive the *Bilcin* growing area
Keep on moving, you will come to the spurting spring
In a hurry fill up your plastic water container
The track will lead you through the open *dhicir* growing area
Do not turn to the infidels (French team) they will persuade you to take forbidden alcohol
Scuttling climb up the opposite slope to the surface of the plateau
Consume your water, the upward slope makes someone sick
They abandoned the site early in the morning
There is no open entrance, the cave site is padlocked
You can pay a short visit to Sahal, and Salaad-Baashe
They slaughter sloppy or shabby women
If you don't look immaculate they may mistake you for the sloppy type
Sahal will attack while others beg for restraint
Fumigate yourself with fragrance and apply perfume
Their lodge is Booj, they retire there in the evening
Follow them and try to walk gracefully
Bootaan Abdi would service your tea and tobacco need
Cusmaan is attractive and would make a good bed-fellow
Saliim is a man of religion, wary but in need of woman
He may refrain from having an affair, but may be seduced to indulge in foreplay
The terrible Mataan would deny you peace
And aggressive Sahal may break your leg in the night
There is no better site in the neighbourhood of Booj
All worldly desires are there for you to stay permanently. (33)

The metaphoric woman is featured in our example as a prostitute. She has been transported in oratory from Jeeni-dheere site to Booj. Mr. Saliim who is sarcastically described in the verse as a man of religion who is more likely to commit the lesser sin of foreplay than of sexual intercourse, took the task of getting rid of the unwanted guest on behalf of his group. To transpose the shame brought by her to another site, Ceel-dibir, Saliim propelled her with a departure verse.

Women stay in numbers in the vicinity of Booj site
Lies must not be told, they gracefully move around in numbers
The youth recite the Prophet's mantle poem and Koran Suras *Ya sin* and *Bara'ah*
There are no morally corrupt youth in our group
Gorgeous woman if you paid us a visit
Bootaan Abdi would sacrifice you in Booj
Set your feet properly on the track, your departure time has come
Never turn to Mr. Siciid, he is sick and not well

Ceel-dibir site has a well where you may take a bath
The residing men are urban if you think they are bedouins
Sumptuously apply yourself with powder and perfume
Jamac spreads out the sleeping blanket in an open ground
Cabdillaahi will operate his thing (penis) inside you
Do not be sloppy, shabby women are disliked. (34)

In this style of poetry, sex is discussed without restraint, notwithstanding the fact that sex is rarely discussed and not in public by rural Somalis. The first verse stigmatises the occupants of Booj as sexually starved. To relieve them of their desire Geedi sends them a prostitute. Such a grave accusation is refuted by Saliim who claimed his unit is morally more pure than the student and urban young brothers residing in Jeeni-dheere. Moreover, if someone fancies a woman, he argues, there are many attractive women in the area. Instead of indulging in sin, Saliim claims they recite the tradition and the Koran.

It is the essence of the verse, not its entertaining diversion on women and sex that is important in order to consider the relative superiority of these poems. Poets and critics scrutinise the essence of the encoded message. A poet who misses the essence of the rival verse and therefore gives a response wide of the mark brings shame to himself and fails his colleagues who share with him both his success and failure.

Apart from its focus on a little discussed subject, sex, this style of poetry presumably acts as a tolerable vehicle where undesirable traits of particular persons are critically exposed. For example, Bootaan Cabdi is portrayed as an inveterate tea drinker and chain smoker of raw tobacco. It is not polite to say such things to a person under ordinary circumstances. On the other hand, the medium could be used to encourage positive qualities of characters who appear in the verse.

Occasionally the generally entertaining and collective spirit of the verse is violated. The competition gets particularised by assuming some form of verbal duel between two antagonistic authors. This has happened between Saliim, the composer of the second verse quoted in the above and a rival, Gabdi. Both of them live in the same village, Galgala.

Saliim composed the first initial inflammatory verse:

You lady who has come from the interior of Nugaal (pastoral region)
Places where no affines reside and the wilderness must not be trodden
You ventured into a bounded territory of useless and poisonous plants *qawlalo* and *ciin*
The generous men no longer reside in the Gadoob region
If you are asking for Cabdi and his colleagues Meyra-gale and Gaban
Take off your underwear before-hand you will undergo something terrible
They have got a grenade and unbreaking object (penis)
They will sumptuously feast you with sorghum bread
There they are residing in a dusty site on the horizontal escarpment
Stay there and do not move to another place until the onset of the *gu'* rains. (35)

Saliim's verse, particularly making fun of the private parts of the rivals, has greatly incensed Cabdi who responded with a terse and threatening short verse:

> If you inquire something of the fundamentals of poetry
> I am a pioneer and have a key to its mastery
> A force (distant kinship relation) that is blind to you is restraining me
> Retreat otherwise I will blind you with a bomb (power of the spoken word). (36)

It is a common feature of confrontation verse, e.g. the "diatribe", to preface it with strong remarks that outline the skill of the poet and his prowess in order to harass and intimidate the opponent. Cabdi's harangue is no exception. He argues that if he were not distantly related to Saliim he would without warning unlease his lethal poem upon him.

To be scared away by the warning shots of an adversary is not the hallmark of a skilled poet. Hence Saliim took no notice of the opponent's banter and harangue. He irrevocably escalated the clash to a level that would have to be settled by a full-blown contest, by making the second attack.

> If you inquire something of the fundamentals of poetry
> I am a pioneer in the art and have a key to its mastery
> Inside my mouth I have got a sharp knife and an iron saw
> I compose unforgettable poems when I confront a non-kin rival
> Retreat otherwise I will blind you with a bomb. (37)

As far as Cabdi was concerned, Saliim's second verse symbolised an act of declaration of verbal war, where words sharper than a knife and iron saw constitute lethal weapons capable of damaging the honour of the looser. Cabdi responded:

> If you have got wisdom, understanding and wit
> You would have avenged those past injuries your head has sustained
> Otherwise you are a family daughter and a marriage partner
> Your hair will plaited while you are waiting for a spouse
> And your reproductive organ would be mine in exchange for bridewealth (camels). (38)

Unlike Saliim's banter and almost empty harangue, Cabdi found a genuine weakness of the opponent which he focused upon. Saliim was assaulted in the past by a youth of a different lineage. He did not avenge the assault. Cabdi capitalised on this point and reduced him to the lowly position of woman, the weak sex, which could be obtained with camels to "beget" children. It is men's responsibility to avenge the blood of women-folk, but a man's noble duty to avenge his own blood from an equal opponent, especially if he belongs to a different lineage.

The damage to honour the spoken word can inflict is most intense, if the accusation made against somebody contains an element of truth. Such is the fate of Saliim. His peers would remember the poem that defamed and designated him as weak as a woman through not avenging his blood. Anyone can cite the poem to embarrass him in a social event.

Desperate to recover some of his status, Saliim composed the last verse in the duel. Instead of attempting to undermine the grave accusation or its total rebuttal, the way he should have responded, he changed the theme by evoking a grey area concerning lineage determination of individual honour and social status.

I am the great architect who put up fences on the four universal corners of the cosmos
I am the originator of the short four lined style of poetry
Those who have a smattering and real experts in poetry fear my skill
And you without a mouth who still milk goats (women's task)
It is rude of you to say a word to man born to aristocratic lineage. (39)

These sector glorification verses clearly indicate the powerful influence of the dominant pastoral culture upon non-pastoral sedentary systems in northern Somalia. To glorify their subsistence economies, frankincense collectors and sedentary cultivators in northern Somalia draw images and metaphors of pastoral provenance. This pastoral outlook was also seen in the preceding chapter on classification of property, where pastoral and non-pastoral property was distinguished.

These styles of poetry, that is sector glorification and the theme of the prostitute woman could be seen to have another crucial implication. They may signify a notion of equality. Since the pastoral economy regards sedentary people as lowly, and in the view of the dominant ideology it is thought that the status of rival economic groups is somehow determined by economic specialisation, non-pastoral groups claim to be of equal standing to pastoralists and, moreover, better in some areas. Thus the egalitarian model of society held by northern Somalis in general seems to be expressed by a levelling view which stresses the strength of the particular economy concerned and denigrates the other.

Since the majority of northern Somalis practise mobile nomadism and women are preferably passed between exogamous lineages to establish affinal links which supplement agnation, it is not surprising that a woman should be chosen as a mobile message-bearer between frankincense stations in Bosaso district. The function of poetry as a cultural element which seeks to enforce equality fits into this context too. The verbal discourse on the prostitute woman is taken up between structurally similar frankincense production units that are of equal socioeconomic standing. The equality and egalitarianism which northerners strongly advocate, holds only for those relations obtaining between the actual frankincense collectors. Relations of economic exploitation obtain between traders and kin client collectors.

CHAPTER SEVEN

The collectivity enterprise of the Siyaad Barre regime

Frankincense development and sales agency

The regime of M. Siyaad Barre that came in power in 1969 aimed to adopt a rapid balanced socialist model of development, the popularly advanced policy of "scientific socialism". This achievement led the regime to try to control the key sectors of the economy, particularly the important banana industry in the south, and the manufacturing and banking systems. For fishing and other areas of production, cooperatives became the sacred scheme for the pursuit of anticipated socialist development and social change. Only stock breeding was excepted: the Livestock Development Agency was set up to initiate processing industries and organise export.

Thus technical ministries initiated and encouraged collective enterprise. For example, the Ministry of Fishing started to organise cooperative fishing communities, while the Ministry of Agriculture did the same to organise the sedentary cultivators. Presumably disappointed with the dismal participation in the cooperative movement by the local producers, the Union of the Somali Cooperative Movement (USCM) was founded on 8 January 1978 as the highest legal authority to consolidate all types of cooperative organisations. Six cooperative organisations grouped into different sectors were brought under the sway of the union:

1. The National Agricultural Cooperative Organisation
2. The National Fisheries Cooperative Organisation
3. The National Organisation of Livestock, Forestry and Incense Cooperatives
4. The National Cooperative Organisation of Handicrafts and Small-Scale Industries
5. The National Organisation of Transport and Construction Cooperatives
6. The National Organisation of Consumer and Service Cooperatives

Apart from the anticipated need for a central authority to handle matters of common interest by the federated organisations, the USCM lacked a coherent strategy. The absence of clearly formulated aims and objectives was most apparent in the legal sphere. The most important legislative measures were law no. 41 of 8 October 1979 and law no. 9 of 18 March 1980. The former regulated the union as the highest legal authority of the cooperative movement, and the latter transferred the management role from the former administering ministries to the USCM.

I participated in the 1985 general assembly of the union held in Mogadishu. Delegates from cooperative organisations presented brief reports often relating to history, organisation, performance and constraints of the respective organisations. Neither the speakers nor the participants questioned cooperativisation in principle, although admirable critical questions were raised. In the face of mounting evidence of inefficiency and bureaucracy of the organisation, union officials promised wide-ranging reforms, by-laws, decentralisation and democratisation of the decision-making process. Besides the genuine need for reform, the anticipated reform strategy was largely designed to impress participating donor agencies who urge the government to liberalise the economy using economic assistance as leverage.[1] To get a general idea about the objectives of the cooperative movement in Somalia, one cannot do better than examine the initial cooperative law, no. 40 of 1973. This, I think, is so far the only comprehensive piece of legislation where the stated objectives of collectivisation, the organisation and responsibility of the hierarchical committees and offices are clearly articulated.

The preface of this amended law describes the aims of the movement. The Somali text idealises "scientific socialism", which is explained as a democratic mass movement and a remarkable achievement of the October Revolution.

In relation to social goals, the movement was thought to liberate the masses from oppression, poverty and exploitation of the capitalist system; particularly emphasised was the need to liberate poor categories of the population engaged in production from the yoke of capitalism. Price regulation of goods and control of the parallel market had been thought to achieve this end.

The movement was assumed to unify and integrate poor sections of society and its exploited middle ranks. These oppressed groups were said to benefit by pooling their power, knowledge and limited material possession to increase production and, by implication, improve their standard of living, and would ultimately contribute to the creation of economy of scale.

The union was acknowledged as a mechanism where technical and scientific methods could be introduced for the productive members of the movement, so that they could improve the quality and increase the quantity of production. Consistent with the socialist policy of industrialisation and processing, the movement would strive to mechanise and process goods produced by the cooperatives. Moreover, making appropriate use of modern scientific and technological achievement, the movement would pursue an import substitution policy and also encourage the export economy.

The USCM was concerned with the appointment of officials for the cooperative organisations, including the frankincense agency and frankincense-producing local cooperatives. It was also an important duty of the union to see that export, and productive activities of the various organisations follow national policy. For instance, frankincense collectors were cooperativised and their produce was purchased and processed for export by the frankincense agency.

Cooperative organisations underwrote the administrative costs of the USCM. In the case of frankincense, this was effected by its regional offices who collected special duties charged on the actual frankincense producers.

The function and organisation of the frankincense agency were discussed in the first chapter. No public organisation to replace the local traders was immediately set up after the banning of the export and handling of

---

[1] For a fuller discussion of the socialist policies in Somalia see Lewis (1988:205–225) and Haakonson (1984).

frankincense by the private sector in 1969. After 3 years of uncertainty during which local traders exported incense illicitly, thus maintaining traditional relations with the actual kin producers of frankincense, in 1972 the government affiliated the frankincense sector with the National Trading Agency. Thus the frankincense sector became a department in the National Trading Agency under the Ministry of Commerce. During the first part of this period cooperativised collectors were required to sell frankincense in only two trading centres, Bosaso in Bari region and Berbera as the closest place for producers in Erigavo region.

From an obscure department in the National Trading Agency, the frankincense agency ascended to an autonomous enterprise in 1981. It expanded by establishing administrative and warehouse installations for storing and processing incense purchased from the collectors in the frankincense-producing districts. Once more in 1981, the agency underwent another reorganisation, ostensibly to induce reform and revitalisation, but I think, primarily as a result of competition between powerful national institutions aspiring to control the hard-currency-generating frankincense sector. A decree transferred the agency from the Ministry of Commerce and placed it under the USCM which was supervised by the Party.

Supplementary working relations of the sort whereby the USCM would provide technical or other forms of required assistance on its own or through collaboration with technical ministries to cooperative organisations were never created. The absence of any significant projects implemented by USCM or the frankincense agency despite many promises testifies to the fact.

Production cooperatives

Northern Somalis seem to have responded positively to cooperativisation largely because it has brought certain incentives, at least in the beginning. They have seen the benefits in the form of loans, food and seed subsidies. Priority of state machinery in the ploughing service with respect to both cooperative land and individual family land have also attracted the few collectivised sedentary cultivators in the northwest region.

The present verse may represent this positive attitude. It was collected from Baargaal village in Alula district, and commemorates the first fair marketing system which was introduced by the then Italian governor in Bari as early as the 1930s, long before the socialist initiatives discussed above.

> Liberated from the past arrangement where one exported his goods unaccompanied
> Liberated from family anxiety resulting from the final declaration "no rubi left"
> Liberated from the inveterate Aden habit of deterred sale and free expedite incense
> God accredited one (the Italian governor) bearing wealth has arrived
> He is the one anticipated by the pauper and the Bedouin
> Applaud and enjoy, before him you were oppressed. (40)

The verse expresses the delight of the gum producers with the marketing organisation (Olibanum Incorporation) that for the first time allowed the collectors direct access to a relatively equitable system operating on the principle of auction. This status is implicitly denied to the local kin traders who previously assumed the marketing of the produce of their kin client producers, and in poetry are described as exploiters.

The verse apparently represents an example of economic considerations being valued more than kinship morality. It is interesting to note a devout Somali poet venerating an "infidel" Italian governor as a God-commissioned hero, because of a marketing reform he implemented.

The collectivisation brought about some instrumental advantages to the collectors, e.g. state subsidies in the form of food and other forms of low interest credits that were made available, albeit temporarily before the 1980s.

Both the pastoral tradition and sedentary economy in northern Somalia are not short of agnatic solidarity. In the former, pastoral kinsmen maintain corporate interests in the camels of the lineage which is reinforced in collective watering and protection of the common herd. In the latter, a man could organise a work party *guus* consisting of cultivating neighbouring kinsmen, for intensive activities like weeding, winnowing, harvesting and sometimes ploughing. However, the experiment in itself failed to take off effectively in the frankincense region of Somalia.

To find the reason for the failure of this enterprise initially created on good will, I will examine some of the factors that undermine the development of a dynamic and viable enterprise. The first concerns the wide-ranging deductions meted out to frankincense collectors. The present verse obtained from Qandala town raises the issue.

Frankincense is as valuable as pearl but I quit because of the difficult system
The numerous exploiting patrons made me quit
Worn to a frazzle by the gruelling work and killing thirst
A clerk had to take charge of my goods induced me quit
Port construction levy and broker charges made me quit
In other instances you (district cooperative committee) act collectively in foray
The disappointing third grade remuneration of Mr Addoosh made me quit. (41)

The aim of the poet who is said to have ceased frankincense collection because of the oppression he experienced, is to try to influence the district cooperative committee, which consists of local elders related to the collectors, to do something about the producer price and the evaluation system. Mr. Addoosh, who is a returnee from Aden and now works as purchase expert for the agency in his home town Qandala, is exhorted to reward kin gatherers with first scale, rather than the disappointing third grade remuneration.

Development toll referred to in the verse as port construction levy is a euphemism for substantial deductions recouped from the actual producers. Regular deductions from the seasonal individual income are within the range of 15–17% of the proceeds from the frankincense sold to the public organisation.

Apart from the regular deductions, other subtle forms of deductions that often escape the attention of casual observers are exacted. At the time of the study, incense collectors surrendered 3 kg of free incense in every 100 kg sold to the organisation. This duty in kind started at 10 kg per 100 kg in some of the districts and was later reduced to half the amount as a result of strong opposition by the producers.

The explanation for the deduction in kind by the organisation officials seems untenable and rather perplexing. It is claimed that the frankincense crop contains some volatile compounds as a result of which it looses some of its weight after some time. Therefore the free payment in kind is argued to compensate for weight reduction of the commodity.

The deduction in kind appears not to be based on accurate calculation of the average weight diminish of the crop in time, but rather founded on vague notions held about the nature of the crop. To penalise the producer for the nature of his product is intensely disturbing. A more suitable alternative entailing no loss of value for the organisation could be to recoup the anticipated weight loss of the goods by revising the price.

As implied in the first chapter, the system of evaluation, including most of the conventional deductions, the grading and processing of frankincense were introduced from Aden. To introduce processing techniques, the Somali government recruited petty traders or brokers in Aden. Most of these traditional experts later worked in the frankincense-producing districts as purchase experts among their lineage groups. Thus the foreign system imposed without significant modification smacks of an undesireable past and oppressive external market conditions, aspects expected by the collectors to be replaced by an impartial national marketing arrangement.

A different form of deduction concerns the jute sacks holding incense. These had been standardised to weigh 2 kg which is deducted from the contents. To observe the quality of the contents and check whether it has been adulterated, the purchaser rips open the side of the sack. The damaged sack is not returned to the collector but taken by the organisation. The practice still existed at the time of the study, despite the USCM prescription to return the sack to its owner.

The range of types of deductions, relatively speaking, are more in Erigavo than in Bosaso district. It is not easy to account for the difference other than to suggest that collectors in Bosaso district are more aware and concerned about the deductions than are their counterparts in Erigavo. In Erigavo, apart from regular and more common deductions, frankincense gatherers are charged the seasonal expenditure of the cooperative committee and purchase personnel as well as other dignitaries who periodically visit production areas for particular duties.

Perhaps more important than the substantial income lost in the form of this bewildering array of deductions, is the crucial factor of price regulation. The following poetic exchange between an accredited incense collector and an elder purchase worker in Qandala district testifies to the importance of the issue. The collector poet spokesman initiated the verbal dual.

> Mr Addoosh you are not a man to be elaborated for the poetic craft
> For a year and more we have been cronies
> I assume that you are a true Somali and a good statesman
> You know as well as I do the plight of incense men
> One trudges to a distant place that normally takes a long time to reach
> One sleeps in a desolate rock station for more than a month
> One abandons his beloved children and herd of sheep
> One struggles to harvest frankincense on plants growing on treacherous cliffs
> If not driven by the desire to get more, no one would have bothered the trouble
> What has been produced and transported with effort is finally brought down for sale in one morning
> And you are anxiously waiting to get it in the market
> You prey for impurities from incense spilled over the floor
> Your rigorous control have wounded the feeling of many patient men
> We swear you in the name of *Saatir* (Allah) and prophetic suras

We entrust you to reward a satisfactory crop with the *prima* scale
And the second best crop with the second scale
Never remunerate us with the lowest third grade, it is absurd. (42)

In the opening first lines, the poet acknowledges some virtues of the purchaser, his skill in the poetic craft, his statesmanship and his intimate knowledge of the difficult conditions in the production of frankincense. Indeed Addoosh was an incense collector early in life. Then he goes on to feature some painful troubles that such work entails, e.g. temporary abandonment of one's guardianship responsibility to family and herd. Finally he strikes his message in the end of the verse by depicting the disappointing purchase practice. He explains the emotional stress that results from the rigorous checks to which goods brought for sale are subjected, as compared to third-grade rewards, a tendency described as absurd and to which the collectors should not be subjected. The response of Addoosh goes:

You have also been prominent, Mr Siciid, in the oral craft
As you have said the two of us understand each other
There are intimate goodwill relations between us
I know as much as you do the plight of incense men
I collected many years from the frankincense field, Sidib-tooxeed
After a long stormy maritime journey with waves splashing all over
A pound of frankincense fetched merely one shilling in the Aden emporium
Yet you were content with such prevailing conditions
Prima and second scale of remuneration are for those who deserve
It is none of your business if the feckless get rewarded with third scale. (43)

The system of frankincense evaluation is largely subjective and never precise. This allows potentially some degree of manipulation. One hears frequent arguments made by the chairmen of the production cooperatives on behalf of the collectors, to purchase experts in the organisation, centring on the quality of marketed goods and the right remuneration.

Sometimes collectors accuse purchasers of favouring their close kinsmen. The organisation officials, especially those in the central office in Mogadishu, accuse purchase experts working in the areas of their ethnic origin of being too generous to their kin producers. Notwithstanding the fact that the system of evaluation would continue to remain loose unless standardised, two reasons underlie such dissenting opinions. The parallel market monopolises the superior grades of frankincense because it pays an attractive price in relation to the official rate. Therefore the agency shows concern over the relatively small quantity of superior grades available to them at the end of the season and the greater quantity their accounts show to have been bought at the first-grade price. Presumably purchase experts try to reward their kin producers for the inferior grades sold to the agency because they are aware of the fact that the government is underpaying the producers.

Frankincense collection areas are for the most part geographically isolated by mountain precipices and remain the most inaccessible and underdeveloped parts of the country. Except in some isolated instances where a water point has been built by the authority in places experiencing acute shortage of water, one finds hardly any useful governmental projects implemented outside the north-eastern port towns.

Schools and health facilities are usually confined to the district towns and some coastal villages. Given the difficult terrain, most of the interior frankincense-producing areas are difficult to reach by motor transport. Small and very slow private fishing launches are improvised to carry goods and people between these vital towns. The government has contributed nothing to the improvement of roads in the frankincense region. It is noteworthy to report that self-help road construction connecting Alula town with frankincense collection areas in the interior ceased in 1985 after the government failed to assist the scheme, as reported by the people.

No technical or scientific methods have been successfully introduced into the sector despite a long history of cooperativisation and the prevailing perception which views traditional methods as deficient and in some ways destructive. After more than a decade of collectivisation, local experts who acquired the knowledge early in life by cultivating incense still conducted the sale transactions of the organisation and supervise the grading system which they introduced from Aden.

Corporate production of frankincense is traditional and precedes modern attempts to initiate cooperation. As explained in the chapter on production, the major unit of frankincense production is a work party consisting of more than one collector. It is fair to say that the movement did not bring about any noticeable impact upon the traditional system of production and organisation. Certainly it has not fostered any superior or more advanced and effective form of solidarity unknown to the collectors.

Cooperativisation neither reduced nor abolished the moralistic issue concerning entrenched relations of economic exploitation between local merchants and kin client producers who often belong to the same corporate lineage. If it has affected such relations in any way this has been to make them more complex and subtle.

Instead of establishing good relations with the producing cooperatives so that fundamental changes could be collectively pursued, one notices a polarisation between the agency and the objects of change. In effect, the enterprise was reduced to a mandatory buying agency which also performed the distribution of inadequate credit facilities.

The enterprise was manipulated to a considerable extent by bureaucrats as a means to advance personal ends. It was a widely reported practice that high-level officials conspired with local traders to allow them to trade in frankincense in contravention of the monopoly. To circumvent official regulation, the authorisation of export transactions through the formal institutions such as the bank, officials in the enterprise allowed incense to be exported. Export permits were given on the justification that the inferior quality which is legal to trade locally is sold to the trader. The trader could pay a hefty commission for the export of the superior incense to the officials concerned.

The commission for superior frankincense was thought to be paid in hard currency, reportedly USD 2–3 per kg. Because of the demand for superior frankincense which could be sold at hard currency prices abroad, it is reported that non-traders with connections enabling them to obtain permits, sold them for profit to interested traders.

Enterprising officials have been accused of stealing frankincense. They recorded goods bought at second grade to have been purchased at first commercial grade. The difference was pocketed.

A merchant authorised to export inferior grades was surreptitiously allowed by the officials to export valuable first grades in exchange for a commission proportionate to the amount of frankincense involved. In a different practice, a certain amount of frankincense was reported spoiled and as having had to be cleared from the store. An equivalent amount of goods in good condition was sold to a merchant, and the spoiled goods were kept in store.

The central authorities were not of course blind to this extensive graft and corruption. To try to limit the scope of public appropriation, district and regional directors of the enterprise and accountants were periodically reshuffled. Some of the notoriously corrupt officials might either be discharged or taken to court for trial. Nevertheless, these malpractices did occur pervasively as they also did in other sectors of the economy.

Of more consequence for the frankincense producers was the administrative tendency to delay payment for the purchased incense, sometimes a delay of up to 8 months was reported. In 1986, it was reported that frankincense collectors in Erigavo district were refusing sell goods to the agency unless the money for the crop was made available. It was not uncommon to see in Mogadishu where the central office for the enterprise was located, district and regional cooperative chairmen waiting for money owed by the enterprise to the local collectors. It is rumoured that the annual budget for buying frankincense was illicitly invested in business for private profit by some prominent officials. This explains partly the lengthy delay of payment.

The organisation's crucial role in providing credits for the collectors was beset by bewildering problems. First, credits were inadequate by all standards, despite the fact that they had considerably increased in amount. For example, the 1984 seasonal credit for Alula district was increased to 6 million SoShs from 600,000 the previous year. Cooperative members and district committee concurred that such a tremendous amount was still inadequate to cover the needs of member collectors.

Second, a systematic method of distributing the available credit was lacking. Cash and occasional food items like sugar, rice, floor and cooking oil, were allocated arbitrarily between the producing districts, and further between local cooperative units engaged in production. Consequently district cooperative chairmen manipulated or rather inflated the total number in their cooperative movement in order to receive a bigger share in the seasonal credit. This caused a disparity of credit distribution among production units, whether this happened by accident or manipulation of influential leaders. In 1984, Alula district in Bari region obtained 6 million SoShs, while Sanaag region which consists of three frankincense-producing districts received 11 million SoShs

Apart from inadequate credit and inappropriate distribution, there seems to have been a lack of appreciation in the enterprise, of the kind of services required by the gatherers. Apart from clothes, utensils and footwear which are needed periodically by the collecting families, basic subsistence household goods like food and everyday items need to be obtained on credit by many collecting families. The period before 1981, when the enterprise was a department in the National Trading Agency which distributed essential goods, is acknowledged by the people as the time when the agency functioned best as a source of credit.

Organisation credits meant for distribution to the frankincense-producing units are claimed to have been invested in private trade for quick profit by some cooperative leaders. In 1984, a former cooperative leader in Erigavo town was paying debt instalments to the organisation. He sold food consignments for his unit of production and then invested the proceeds in exported livestock. The animals were sold at a loss and the cooperative leader became insolvent.

However, the record of the agency is not all negative. As a matter of fact, it also accomplished some useful things in the course of time. In its earlier period only two purchase and processing offices, Berbera and Bosaso, operated in the frankincense territory. During my fieldwork all districts owned administrative and processing facilities that were easily accessible to the collectors. Organisation vehicles, though limited and totally lacking in some districts, transported goods from remote production areas to collection villages in places where usable tracks exist. Collectors using organisation vehicles were charged fuel cost, but many of them claimed that in the past they were charged the total transport cost for a free service. The most important achievement of the nationalisation of the frankincense sector was though the creation of processing and grading techniques introduced from Aden to Somalia.[2]

The role of middle-men in the cooperative enterprise

The resilience of the private sector is a distinctive feature of the frankincense economy. Instituted marketing organisations often fail to disrupt traditional relations of exploitation between local traders and client producers. Food loans and other forms of credits have been necessary for the herd-poor collectors. The ability of the local merchants to provide such facilities compared to public organisations seems to have promoted the maintenance of the traditional unbalanced relations between local traders and kin collectors.

Generally speaking, local merchants as rural intellectuals and intermediaries between their social groups and the government, installed themselves in the movement. In response to the policy of cooperativisation, each merchant mobilised his kinsmen to appoint him as their chairman.

At the time of the study, more than two thirds of the cooperative district chairmen in the two frankincense regions, Bari and Sanaag, were merchants engaged, to a lesser or greater degree, in import–export trade. Many of them had themselves cultivated frankincense early in life before they migrated to towns. Although they resided in the district towns, they maintained ties with their rural kin collecting groups.

Given the failure of the enterprise to effect anticipated socioeconomic changes, it became a mandatory buying body and the source of insufficient and unreliable credit. As a source of credit and a marketing organisation, it resembled traditional traders who provided credits, and to a large degree, especially in early times, exported the seasonal incense produce of their kin client producers. Cooperative committees, which actually were the same as local traders, seem to have corresponded to the local intermediaries *muqadin* between traders and producers.

The function of middle-men in establishing a link between the micro and macro level of interaction was effected in various ways. One of these was their capacity to understand, communicate and interpret government decisions to cooperativised lineage groups involved in frankincense production.

---

[2] See chapter one.

To facilitate free access for tenant collectors, in the early 1970s the government decreed frankincense to be public property. The decision was interpreted as a rejection of tradition, mostly by influential middle-men, many of them having rights over frankincense fields. Because of ensuing strong resistance which is said to have resulted in a total confrontation between landless and right-holding agnates, the government retreated by not forcing the decision which subsequently degenerated to a dead log.

Middle-men escorted government officials in rural areas inhabited by their kin groups. Cooperative chairmen who were mainly traders organised the feasts that were provided for the visiting dignitaries. It was middle-men who were honoured even if in most cases the cost was afterwards distributed among the kin groups. The merchant, in turn, often acted as one of the prominent spokesmen of the community, and could elaborate some of the official views that might have required further explanation.

Merchants were doing better than the public enterprise as a source of credit. Apart from the fact that interest on state credit was comparatively low, these facilities were often inadequate and unreliable. They often reached the recipients too late. It is quite apparent that these services were not at all tuned to satisfy the wide-ranging needs of the collecting families.

Concerning the seasonal credit account of a particular collector in Bosaso district, an example, obtained from the district cooperative chairman who was a merchant based in both Bosaso town and Galgala village, illustrates the point (Table 5).

It is doubtful whether a modern enterprise would be able to operate such a complex and comprehensive credit service from community stores in rural areas. The actual collector, his wife or indeed any other dependent person could receive a required item on credit from different local traders based in different villages, all of them passing on credit to the district chairman whose personal influence allowed such a system operate.

There is also another advantage in credit facilities provided by the traders: they are much more flexible than were those of the enterprise. In many cases collectors fail to repay all the debt and local merchants do not usually withdraw credit from indebted clients but mainly offer them a running credit. The indebted is pressed to work hard to be able to settle the debt. In an extreme case the merchant may demand the indebted kin to sell some animals to pay the debt.

Members of Hodmo cooperative branch in Erigavo district reported that, in 1984, kin merchant leaders organised the movement by paying membership fees on behalf of their clients, without bothering to create a central fund obtained from members, as the rules require. Once they had submitted the fund to the concerned authority to convince it that the recommended reorganisation of the movement has been carried out, they withdrew their deposits which they needed for private investment.

In Iskushuban district, there occurred a proportionately greater corruption involving embezzlement of the central fund of the cooperative. Out of the total 8-year subscription fund, estimated by the new chairman at about 1,650,000 SoShs, only 3,000 SoShs were found in the central fund by the newly-appointed committee in 1984. This enormous misappropriation of public wealth is believed to have continued for the whole period of 8 years with the alleged connivance of the district authority.

From the above, it can be understood how the limitations of the organisation as a source of credit and as a marketing board led to the dominance of middle-men in the sector. Cooperative leaders were quick to blame the frankincense agency for all the existing problems.

Table 5. *Seasonal credit account of a collector*
Name of the collector: Muse Cige

DATE	DESCRIPTION OF THE CREDIT	VALUE SoShs
7.4.80	12 quintal of rice and 1 quintal of flour	700
18.6.80	Cash obtained from Xuseen in Galgala	20
17.8.80	Debit by Faarax Caddeysin	279
11.9.80	Debit by Faarax Caddeysin	318
29.9.80	12 quintal of rice obtained from Faarax Cabdi	320
11.10.80	2 kg of sugar obtained from Faduma Ciise	20
4.11.80	Debit by Faarax Caddeysin	?
6.11.80	Cash obtained from Xussen	20
8.11.80	Cash obtained from ?	200
13.11.80	Cash drawn by his wife	18
19.11.80	Cash obtained from Axmed Gurxan	200
10.2.81	1 quintal of poor quality rice	584
10.2.81	Seasonal frankincense field rent	120
27.3.81	Debit by Axmed Jaamac	312
Total		**3435**
Total value of frankincense sold to the enterprise		2350
Balance, debit		1085

Enterprise officials are claimed to have been insensitive to the plight of the collectors, and they are accused of lacking proper understanding of the prevailing conditions. Local merchants, on the other hand, claimed that they fulfilled essential services for the collecting members of their kin groups. They acted as chairmen of the cooperative production units and sources of reliable credit, a system made easier by the inadequate state facilities they administered. They were also regional traders who engaged in the parallel market. As the data seem to suggest, both local merchants and enterprise officials had a tendency to manipulate the movement for economic ends. Middle-men involved directly in the administration of the cooperatives, as well as many others, collaborated subtly with the district and regional government officials in the informal frankincense market which integrated the interests of all these particular groups.

The parallel market

As in many developing countries, the informal economy had not received serious attention as an important economic category in Somalia before the 1980s. Vali Jamal (1987) has argued that the Somali economy could be considered as unconventional since a substantial part of the economic activities elude government control and escape the national account. Remittances from Somali workers abroad which are repatriated through informal channels are thought to represent a greater portion of the national economy; export and import trade to a considerable extent operate at free market exchange rates outside state control; similarly the bulk of internal trade also escapes government control.

Jamal examines the implications of the pervasive parallel economy and other features of the Somali economy for important indicators like welfare. Given the extent of the informal economy, estimates which suggest that the unofficial private trade handled about 80% of the total value of the frankincense trade seem not to be unfounded. Private trade dominated frankincense exports, because it paid relatively better and attracted superior and most valuable chewing grades of *meydi* exported to Saudi Arabia.

The 1985 price for 1 kg of first grade *meydi* incense was about 330 SoShs compared to 1,000 SoShs on the parallel market. The selling price of the organisation for the same amount in the same year was USD 35 (3,125 SoShs). The figures illustrate the big margin between the producer price and the real value of the crop.

Under such circumstances, the market strategy of the frankincense collectors was to try to sell most of the expensive superior *meydi* grades to the private traders for good prices, and the inferior *meydi* grades and cheaper *beeyo* frankincense to the public enterprise.

If organisation officials asked the collectors what they had done with the valuable chewing grades of *meydi* types of frankincense, they received a diplomatic answer. Over-exploitation of the species, inadequate rainfall and other extraneous factors disturbing production were often quoted as reasons for the low proportion of the superior quality frankincense sold to the enterprise.

The higher price of the parallel market can be said to have benefited the collectors in other ways apart from its positive effect on income. Unofficial trade instigated a beneficial competition and price war between the official enterprise and enterprising local traders. Several times during the course of this study the agency found it necessary to increase the official producer price to try to get a share in the trade of superior qualities. For example, in 1985 the price of 1 kg of first grade *meydi* incense was increased from 60 to 330 SoShs. The parallel market price had correspondingly increased from 220 to 1000.

What gave the informal frankincense trade a dynamic momentum and pervasive tendency, was its capacity to combine and integrate the interests of various groups: those of the client collectors and local kin traders or middle-men together with those of the officials of the enterprise as well as district and regional officials.

Ironically, the pivotal link in the operation of the informal trade was assumed by the cooperative leaders themselves. As leaders of the frankincense producers, they effected the crucial initiation link between traders and kin collectors. Transactions might be completed in their presence. The price and details of the quality and quantity of goods that could be made available by the collectors were settled.

Traders who inhabit district or regional towns may leave the production area after the transaction is concluded. The exchange of goods and money is accredited to the closest kinsman residing in the area. In the absence of a close relative, like a brother, a cousin or an uncle, it is sufficient just to be a member of the same *dia*-paying group. Cooperative leaders obtained commission from the contact they established between producers and traders.

There are no conspicuous bosses among the dealers operating the informal frankincense trade. Most of them are local merchants dealing with collecting members of their lineage groups in their own territory. Some are small-scale traders aspiring to become wealthy ones. The details of the agreement varies from one area to another. In some areas a certain amount of frankincense is sold to the trader and a portion is consigned to him, so that he will bring back to the clients the value of the consigned goods in hard currency or consumer goods. It is also common to sell the goods to the trader for a good price.

In some isolated towns like Alula where traded foodstuffs are sometimes scarce, people seem to think that they should be given special treatment by the government. In the absence of such treatment, they feel neglected and consequently use local frankincense resources in a way useful to the people in the district. Such grievances are exploited by merchants who urge collectors to sell frankincense to them, in order to make it possible for them to import essential goods needed by the collectors.

Agnation is used to handle illicit trade. Local traders claim that they are unfairly treated in terms of obtaining official permits for export of inferior frankincense and <u>Commiphora</u> gums that are freely traded. To circumvent this, they illicitly trade frankincense produced in their areas of ethnic origin.

Outsiders participate in the frankincense trade chiefly through formal channels and do not meddle in the parallel trade for good reasons. First, they lack adequate knowledge about types and qualities and may easily be deceived. I heard many stories about ignorant traders who were sold inferior goods. Related to this is the fact that they are not acquainted with the collectors and therefore cannot act directly without a local intermediary. Second, they are liable to be reported to the authorities.

In general, export is executed in two alternative ways. A merchant or a representative of a syndicate with a common interest in the goods being illicitly exported, travels to the final destination abroad, Djibouti or Aden. A motor launch is hired there. It is escorted back to one of the numerous natural harbours on the northeastern Red Sea coast where goods are made ready for a quick haul. The merchandise is hauled aboard the vessel during the night.

This kind of nocturnal operation was relatively cheap since it avoided the hefty commission usually paid to the government officials. However, it posed some difficulty. Somalis are very communicative and the news about the operation soon filtered out to the authority. The district authorities were antagonised and the future interests of those concerned undermined. Therefore, the second option became more feasible: A merchant negotiated secretly with the important officials, the commissioner, the party representatives, security and police chiefs and others. He sought their implicit permission for exchange of an agreed commission, depending upon the quality and quantity of frankincense.

As stated above, sometimes the legal system acted as an umbrella for the parallel trade. A merchant permitted to export low quality products was allowed to export better quality goods, or an amount exceeding the permitted quantity. This happened with the knowledge of the enterprise officials and government departments responsible for export control.

The foregoing is, however, just an outline of the prevailing pattern, and should not convey the idea that all officials are corrupt or that the central authority was oblivious to the economic offences taking place. To glimpse a heavy-handed example concerning the central government's attempt to curtail such economic mismanagement, prominent district and other officials in Alula were called to report in Mogadishu in 1984. None of them returned to the district to resume his responsibility and some were demoted, as a result of large-scale frankincense trafficking in the district. However, such occasional crack-downs on corruption are not sufficiently frequent to contain any tendency.

Apparently there seems to be a stake for all the interest groups that participated in the parallel frankincense trade. However, bigger chunks went to the more powerful groups, the middle-men and the government officials. The actual producers derived the least benefit from it.

The relatively small benefit derived by collectors in the parallel market is not often realised without some negative consequences. On those occasions when the central authority pushed the local government, patrols were dispatched to frankincense production areas, and some of the collectors were intimidated and harassed. For example, in 1983, a group of about thirty frankincense collectors were reported to have started to unpack the convoy of camels and donkeys near a collecting site not far from the main road, so that the goods could be transported from there on by the organisation vehicle to Iskushuban district town. All of a sudden an approaching truck fired a hail of bullets in their direction. The majority fled for their lives. They returned to the nomadic hamlets where they reported that the goods had been robbed by armed dissidents. The assumed robbery by dissidents was made in association with a repulsed attack on Iskushaban town which took place shortly before the incident. The invading truck turned out to be carrying police and militia who were misinformed about the real intention of the convoy. A local employee of the organisation reported that the convoy was destined for trafficking, according to some informants, to create trouble for some of the collectors against whom he had a grudge. Those who stayed with the goods were rounded up and taken to Iskushuban town. After rigorous interrogation no suspicious intention was found, and the goods and collectors were released.

I was told of several cases where cooperative leaders were detained by the district authority, presumably to impress a visiting high-level delegation, and freed by the delegation who understood the circumstances. Several innocent victims of perverted justice were considerably released by the party chairman of the Union of the Somali Cooperative Movement during his 1984/85 tours in the frankincense region.

There is no distinct criterion to assess what sort of goods under certain circumstances should be considered illicit in the official view of the matter. I know many instances where frankincense consignments claimed to be destined for the organisation were caught in the middle and charged with contraband offences. Some suspicious circumstances cannot be ruled out, and the usual justification by hoarders in villages, following a police search, that the recovered goods were destined for official sale are not all genuine. Nevertheless, the issue of careless arrests in grey circumstances must be a matter of crucial concern.

In their reports prepared for the central authority, government officials naturally conceal their economic interest in the illicit frankincense trade. They recite a characteristic litany suggesting physical and logistical obstacles that are said to impede effective control of the tendency. The proximity of the mountainous frankincense region which is difficult to penetrate to the coast which is endowed with natural harbours was often given as one of the important factors facilitating the trade. Limited police forces, lack of speed boats to guard the extensive coast, inadequate communication facilities, the price incentive and the entrenched relations between traders and bonded kin collectors, were some of the other factors suggested to promote the lucrative informal trade. In reality most interest groups favoured the persistence of the trade because of vested economic interests. Hence the incumbent obstacles raised by the officials as promoting factors were merely scapegoat mechanisms employed to try to cloak their collusion with middle-men and the frankincense collectors.

The collusion of the government officials in the syndicated parallel trade, may be indicated by the insignificant record relating to the number of offenders who were actually convicted of trafficking. In Alula district in 1976, following a high level judicial inquiry, four motor boats were confiscated, fifteen offenders consisting of small-scale traders and middle-men were sentenced from 15–30 years and fined between 20–30,000 SoShs. Despite short-term detention of some suspects, no one is known to have been tried for trafficking offences in the district after that year despite the existence of the informal trade.

In the neighbouring Qandala district, I was told, 144 kg of frankincense was retrieved from a hideout in a desolate village near Qandala town. This represents the only catch that has been classified as contraband in the records. It was accidentally found by high-school leavers doing national service. In other frankincense-producing districts, court cases involving large-scale trafficking were insignificant compared to the scale of the practice.

Transformation in access to frankincense: from share-cropping to rent

We have seen in the foregoing, how the cooperative experiment fell victim to the manipulation of the powerful forces of middle-men and government and enterprise officials for economic ends. The actual frankincense collectors for their part, participated in this perverted scheme of development by selling part of their produce in the informal market which acted as an arena for combining these various economic interests. Given the absence of an effective organisation to seek some orderly and just transformation, and the need to transform some of the traditional relations with respect to access in the frankincense property, incense men manipulated relations of production at the local level.

In terms of access to the primary resource, the most important transformation has been a tendency towards a rental arrangement instead of the traditional share-cropping. This process appears to have progressed not by the force of statutory rules, but chiefly by the will of landless people to improve their conditions. Tenant collectors started to refuse share-cropping and the trend swung towards a tenancy system based on seasonal rent which determines access to the exploitation of jointly-owned frankincense property.

This important transformation may be considered to have thoroughly succeeded in the frankincense-producing districts in Bari region, albeit that share-cropping in a modified form still exists in some local areas. Thus the substance of the arrangement is remarkably different from its precedent. In Karkaar area between Iskushuban and Qardho, the total value of the seasonal yield is divided into three parts, not unlike the traditional scheme. One portion is automatically received by the producer or producers. The remaining two amounts are first deducted from the seasonal joint production investment. The balance is then equally divided between the collectors and the owners. Herein lies the improvement of the system. One share which used to be the prerogative of the right-holders in the past is now shared equally between tenant collectors and the owners.

In general, the neighbouring Sanaag incense region appears far behind in terms of the transcendence of tenancy over share-cropping. The reasons are difficult to identify other than conjecture that collectors are less dynamic and more traditional than their counterparts in Bari. A similar process of share-cropping modification has taken place in areas where it still exists.

The emergent share-cropping system in Erigavo district is known as *kala-badh*, "two equal halves". The total value of the seasonal output is first recouped from the production expenditure. The balance is then divided on an equal basis between the producers and the right-holders.

As explained in connection with the ownership relations, the right-holders would like to maintain the status quo since it affords them one third of the value of the produce. But as it is getting difficult to maintain, they have opted for a form of distribution which is less beneficial than the traditional one but more advantageous than the buoyant rental scheme.

To exemplify how the share-cropping system in its modified form benefits the owners more than the rental arrangement, let us consider an average incense field. Two frankincense collectors may produce goods valued at about 60,000 SoShs in a season. Suppose the costs of production net at about 15,000 SoShs. In terms of the two part division that is current in Erigavo district, the owners and labourers would each receive 22,500 SoShs. If the right-holders rent such an incense field growing *yagcar* species that yields the expensive *meydi*, they may not obtain from it more than 5,000 SoShs in a season.

The example explains a collector's desire to enter rental arrangements with owners. Due to scarcity or unyielding demand of the right-holders of a good field, those who have no alternative other than to labour in a share-cropping scheme, resort to commonplace deceptive means aimed at reducing the amount they actually pay to the owners. They lower the seasonal output and keep the underdeclared amount which may be sold in the parallel market for their benefit.

Title-holders are aware that they are being deceived by landless collectors, as production capacity of frankincense fields in an average year is commonplace knowledge. In both serious rhetoric and casual discussion, incensed owners often threaten to evict deceitful tenants from the property, and to exploit it themselves. Such aspiration, however attractive due to the increased value of the crop, is to date not practical for most owners. They often lack surplus labour from herding which may conveniently be deployed in the production of frankincense.

In a world of crumbling traditional means of distribution, and in the absence of an effective modern organisation to assume this function, owners promote their interests through the rent institution. In areas where share-cropping had become virtually obsolete, owners have tremendously increased the rent.

Incense men reasonably expect some increase in the rent because of the increased international value of frankincense. But they are disturbed by exorbitant increases from some owners who seem to have an eye on the price of the crop in the parallel market. In various places across the frankincense region, cases where owners have demanded the rent to be paid in kind have been reported. The object of this disguised share-cropping is to obtain a certain amount of goods which may be sold in the parallel market to earn an income exceeding that accruing from the rent.

The official policy of the 1980s aiming to abolish share-cropping and tenancy arrangements had very little impact. The factors accounting for the failure are the tenacity of tradition and the opposition of the owners, particularly influential middle-men, many of whom are right-holders and whose support is essential for the laws to have any chance. Both enterprise and government officials lacked the incentive or necessary resources for a sustained effort to implement this unpopular decision in the most difficult and isolated part of the country.

Alula district shows what happens in the case of imposed administrative regulation of access to the owned frankincense property. Share-cropping is relatively unknown in this very poor and remote district. Cooperative leaders in the district started to regulate the exploitation of the property. The legal basis for the intervention was cited as a decree formulated by the then deputy chairman of the party responsible for the cooperatives on 23 May 1979. Point 9 of the decree calls for prosecution of any offender who asserts rights over frankincense property or else demands a rent from it or commits any other offence that is contrary to the stability of the sector.

Themselves experts of tradition, and realising the slim chance of abolishing rights standard, cooperative leaders took a middle of the road course. To strike a balance between antagonistic title-holders and tenants, they implicitly acknowledged the rights of the holders by allowing them to obtain regulated rent without further interference.

Apart from the disappointment which followed the regulated rent, owners strongly objected to a different injunction demanding the registration of frankincense fields against the landless-exploiting collectors in lieu of the absentee holders. To control and increase production and also to limit trafficking has been given as the underlying aim. Understandably the strategy pleased tenants and antagonised owners. The controversy instigated an intense public debate focusing on which tenure system, prescriptive rights versus free access, was suitable for the protection and exploitation of the commercial forests.

On the one hand, owners were volubly warning against the adverse consequences of communalisation of the property. They claimed that free access would prompt indiscriminate and careless exploitation which would endanger the valuable plants. On the other hand, the supporters of communalisation dismissed the argument. They stated that it was not beneficial for anyone with long-term vested interest in the property to inflict damage to the property by applying damaging methods. Tenant collectors claimed to know the cultivation methods better than chiefly absentee owners, some of them being townspeople who have never actually seen their inherited frankincense fields growing in the country of their lineage groups.

To play the rules, some holders started to seriously consider cultivating frankincense in order to put their names against their property. Tenant collectors made fun of villagers who had not ventured into the interior, asking whether they could face the hardship of collection.

The protection of the frankincense groves is an important and delicate matter that has to be carefully handled. The local discord can be inflated and manipulated to suit the divergent claims of the disputing kinsmen. To give free access to landless collectors is morally attractive but falls short of an alternative effective tenure system. It raises the question of responsibility for the protection of the property.

The issue has social implications which concern the obvious interest in the land and the valuable commercial species it grows. The majority of tenant collectors in the Alula district belong to the numerically dominant lineage group. Some of its landless collectors rent fields which belong to members of the traditionally aristocratic lineage and their minority allied or related groups. The dominant group, with insufficient resources for its members and chiefly depending upon collection, believes that in the past the relatively resource-rich aristocratic lineage and its affiliates dominated the district affairs prior to the Siyaad Barre government.

The out-migrated and largely non-cultivating aristocratic groups claim that the dominant group was motivated to dispossess them of their customary property by capitalising on the socialist government's policy of equality and social justice. This was assumed to be the real purpose of the reform policy pursued by the district cooperative committee which was dominated by members from the numerically dominant group.

In most of the other districts, where statutory rules had been ignored and thus tradition prevailed, we witness escalation of rent and modified share-cropping. On the contrary, in Alula where an attempt to control rent was made, rents were lower, which in turn promoted social schisms.

When looking back into the cooperative era in the frankincense sector of Somalia, numerous dysfunctional factors that constrained the development of a modern and efficient enterprise can be noted: deductions, delayed payment, price regulation, insufficient and inadequate distribution of credit facility, not to mention endemic corruption in the enterprise. Corruption and graft as well as inefficiency, perpetuated by the middle-men, were chiefly responsible for the failure of the movement. Relations of economic exploitation existed between frankincense collectors and local merchants who provided credits for their kin client producers already prior to the Siyaad Barre regime. Such unbalanced relations were then maintained in subtle forms in the framework of the cooperative enterprise. Cultural elements intrinsic in the social organisation may also have had implications for the development of the movement. Nevertheless, I think that inefficiency and imbalanced economic relations represent the most important factors restraining the development of modern enterprise in the Somali case.

CHAPTER EIGHT

Conclusions

Property classifications in frankincense production

This study has examined the production and marketing of frankincense in northern Somalia from a number of perspectives: cultural, sociological, economic and political. To conclude, I wish to draw together the principal findings, under the broad headings of property, poetry and political economy.

Somalis classify wealth into two broad categories, animate and inanimate or pastoral and non-pastoral. Pastoral wealth consists of domestic species of camels, sheep and goats, horses, donkeys and mules, whose services are required to varying degrees for animal husbandry. Inanimate property is a residual category which distinguishes domestic stock from other useful properties, e.g. money, jewellery and gold, land and agricultural products, weaponry, trucks, building property, enterprise etc.

Different values are attached to the different stock raised by Somalis. Partly because as drought animals they can be relied upon in harsh times, camels are the most cherished pastoral herds. In addition, they have social and symbolic importance which transcends those of the less sturdy sheep and goats and cattle. They are ceremoniously passed between social groups on important occasions like marriage and homicide compensation.

Many corporate activities of the pastoral Somalis revolve around the camel. They are collectively defended, jointly watered from the deep wells by close agnates, and jointly raided, particularly in the past. To reinforce collective interest over these herds whose production and prosperity depends much upon corporate function, camels are symbolised in various ways as group property. Camel herds of individual members of the lineage usually bear a lineage brand, unlike the other stock of sheep and goats which bear the brand of the individual owner.

At birth, a father gives his son a female camel known as *xuddun xidh*, "navel knot", which forms the nucleus of the future herd of the young man. Women do not inherit camels, though they may inherit cash, buildings and other urban property, as well as some small stock. Camels are commonly passed from father to son, in effect through men of the patriline.

Because of their practical, social and symbolic values, camels are prestigious animals which Somalis cherish and avidly accumulate. Unlike the small stock, they are rarely given in assistance to kinsmen, and most herders exclude their camels from the payment of the annual Islamic taxation on property. The different values in relation to the different species is aptly expressed by the designation of the camel herds as the "permanent pastoral wealth", and the contrasting view which signifies the small stock as "consumer goods". Unlike hoarded camels, small stock of sheep and goats are frequently slaughtered for guests, offered as gifts to kin, and are often sold for cash which is exchanged for grains and other domestic goods.

Of all the pastoral stock, the Somali pony was traditionally the most valuable. As an instrument of warfare, its essential role in the protection of the lives and property of pastoral people in a turbulent pastoral world gave it this elevated status which it has lost in modern times.

Although pastoralists attach different values to the different stock, nevertheless, the pastoral model of property classification is not unexpectedly biased against non-pastoral property. Domestic stock and their products are thought to be superior to agriculture and agricultural products. Pastoralists despise agriculture and consider it as a lowly occupation which is taken up by someone destitute in herds. Their view of fishing is even more degrading. They tend to describe fishing as "maritime hunting", in an attempt to reduce it to hunting that is regarded proper for marauding beasts and not an appropriate human occupation.

Not unlike camel herds which are idealised as lineage property, sedentary resources of frankincense forests and agricultural land are also regarded as community wealth. Like camels, in order not to allow such basic properties to circulate between groups, women who pass between distant and often antagonistic lineages in marriage are not allowed to inherit them. What may be said to differentiate sedentary properties from camels is that frankincense and agricultural fields are a fixed and generally unexpanding wealth. Hence, they do not usually circulate between different lineages and within the members of a particular lineage. Camels on the other hand, though coveted and avidly accumulated, are ceremoniously passed between social units on important occasions, such as marriage and compensation.

The pastoral attitude towards urban properties, e.g. money and estate, is ambiguous. Such urban wealth may be coveted but generally it is considered artificial, less reliable and less permanent than rural properties of pastoral herds and land. Due to the overwhelming commitment of pastoralists to herds, and the tremendous influence of the pastoral culture pivoted on camels upon non-pastoral groups in Somalia, there seems to be a general tendency to reduce other types of properties to pastoral wealth. In both rural and urban areas, it is usually the case that blood compensation is conveniently valued in terms of camels. Since it is not practical to effect compensation in actual camels between lineages concerned, a sum calculated on contractual camel price which is much lower than the real value of the camel is paid.

Frankincense trees and agricultural crops are classified as non-pastoral wealth. Frankincense people and sedentary cultivators may aspire to own camels. However, they consider commercial forests, land and crops, as their respective share in Allah's just distribution of basic community resources between social groups. Surprisingly, in the sector glorification rhetoric, sedentary groups draw extensive analogies between sedentary resources and cherished camels which act as a value standard. Moreover, sedentary groups point out certain advantages their system has over the overarching pastoral way of life. This can be considered as being both due to an innocuous eccentric glorification of the community resources and a defence against the domineering pastoral culture.

The poetry of frankincense production

Elaborate and extensive oral poetry holds a prominent position in the culture of the Somali society. Further it features to a great extent in the more encompassing cultural elements of pastoralism and Muslim belief and practice. Accordingly, important historical, philosophical and religious issues are committed, preserved and transmitted through this medium.

Notwithstanding some structural and technical information on the Somali language in general, most studies on poetry dilate upon the political dimension of the art, quite often clan politics. This limited scholarly attention inspired me to look briefly into the subject. The wider social functions of the craft which have not been systematically explored so far, and the richness of the ethnographic material, account for my interest in the subject and its utilisation in this study.

The skill of the composer, impressive style and high linguistic standard, are important qualities both critics and wider public audiences admire in the poetic craft. However, the essence of the medium basically lies in its "social connotation". Thus Somalis compose poems for all sorts of purposes: to solemnise national and local matters, and for any other legitimate personal or corporate social, political or economic function. Not surprisingly, the generally egalitarian pastoral Somali appear not to set encumbrances for the participation in this popular public discourse. Thus, revered community and national poets come from all walks of life and do not necessarily emerge from a particular social or economic stratum.

The poetry of the frankincense production reflects the antagonism between rival economic groups in northern Somalia. An element of comparison and denigration of one economic group or another testifies to this tendency. Not unlike other economic groups, frankincense collectors draw images and metaphors from the superordinate pastoral culture in the glorification of their exploits. This further corroborates the pastoral outlook of the Somalis.

Poet spokesmen of frankincense collectors describe frankincense property to be as economically important as herds are. Commercial resin which buys the collector essential goods is compared to camel's milk which sustains the life of the pastoralist. In the sector glorification theme, advantages of one sector over a rival one are emphasised. Thus, the frankincense economy is represented as flawless and free from pastoral restraints. Commercial frankincense forests do not browse, nor do they depend upon scarce drinking water resources, as do pastoral herds. To distinguish the valued semi-settled pattern of the collectors from the erratic nomadic movements, frankincense property is designated as fixed. And the long-standing commercial culture of the frankincense crop is a point on which collectors claim their economy excels over the recently commercialised livestock sector.

The competition for excellence between antagonistic economic groups in northern Somalia is often carried out between a particular group and the dominant pastoral system. Representing frankincense as a superior economy in relation to herding seems to contradict a parallel representation in which other local economic groups draw metaphors and images from the superordinate pastoral culture which acts as a standard of value for Somalis regardless of economic specialisation. In one context, valuable frankincense forests are represented as more important than camel herds. In another context, through the same poetic media, camels are subordinated to frankincense.

The sector oratory not only acts as a public forum for the glorification of the group resource, but the craft is also used as an expression for the constraints and endemic problems of the economy concerned. For instance, the praise verses which exalt frankincense are replaced with lament verses denouncing the occupation as daunting, less rewarding and ultimately miserable. This ambivalent attitude towards the primary resource of the community is a general tendency notable among northern Somalis. Cultivators in the northwest region both glorify and denigrate farming. The demanding task of agricultural work is justified by a local belief which reckons farming as a punishment imposed upon sedentary groups in general, and due to original sin.

Using herds as a standard for economic excellence, cultivators in the northwest region, like frankincense collectors, exalt crops to the rank of camels. At euphoric moments of sector glorification, venerated pastoralism becomes subordinated to farming which is fulsomely adulated.

Antagonism between specialised economic groups is fundamentally based upon competition for land and water resources. Opposition between specialised groups does not entirely coincide with lineage organisation. A considerable number of cultivating families in the northwest region practise nomadism; similarly, many members of the frankincense-producing lineages in the frankincense region engage in pastoralism. Presumably antagonism between economic groups is most intense when lineage ties and economic specialisation coincide.

At the highest level, the boundary of opposition could be drawn between the superordinate pastoral culture and relatively localised sedentary systems. Because of uncritical dependence upon the pervasive pastoral lifestyle for metaphors and images suitable for the glorification of their economies, sedentary cultivators and frankincense collectors reduced themselves to localised economies struggling for survival and identity in the framework of an overarching pastoral culture.

The dramatisation of sex and women is said to be one of the distinctive features of the theme about the imagined prostitute in Bosaso district. Sex and prostitution which puritanical Somalis shrink from discussing in public, are openly discussed in this style of poetry by rival poets working in an area of frankincense production. It is suggested that this acts to discourage undesirable qualities of characters who appear in the verse by critically exposing bad behaviour. It may also be used as a medium to encourage positive qualities of characters who appear in the verse.

Sector glorification poems and the theme about the prostitute may also be said to signify a notion of equality. The overarching pastoral economy considers sedentary as lowly. In the view of the dominant ideology it is held that the status of rival groups is determined by economic specialisation, non-pastoral groups seem to claim to be of equal standing and better in some areas. Thus, the egalitarian model held by pastoral Somalis regardless of economic specialisation seems to be expressed by a levelling view which stresses the strength of a particular economy concerned and the denigration of the other.

Marriage patterns may explain the reason why a woman is chosen as a mobile metaphoric message-bearer between rival poets residing in neighbouring stations. In general, northern Somalis practise lineage exogamy to establish affinal links which supplement agnation which provides the basis for important corporate functions (Lewis 1962c).

The function of sector glorification poems in search of further equality applies here as well. The verbal discourse on the prostitute is taken up between structurally similar frankincense production units that are of equal socio-economic standing. In the frankincense economy, the egalitarian folk model held by northern Somalis is only true with respect to relations obtaining between the actual collectors. The study shows relations of economic exploitation between frankincense collectors and related middle-men.

Apparently the sexual joking theme of the prostitute enshrines an element of religion which relates to the sexual morality of Islamic society. Prostitution and immoral sex are proscribed and therefore seldom occur in the rural areas in Somalia.

The political economy in frankincense production

Since colonial times, successive governments have been concerned about entrenched relations of economic exploitation obtaining between local merchants and kin collectors. Understandably this offered a moral justification for concerned governments to try to reduce exploitation, often by establishing short-lived, less exploitative marketing boards which were also thought to improve efficiency. Such strategies of the colonial and succeeding civilian governments have been suggested to indicate a static model of development which resembles a pendulum oscillating between instituted marketing organisations and a resolute private sector that emerged after the failure of each initiative.

The prevailing tendency of rental and share-cropping arrangements between landless collectors and right-holders, testifies to the unbalanced distribution of the community property that took place in the nineteenth century in Bosaso region and in the beginning of the twentieth century in neighbouring Erigavo. Lack of consensus on the initial partition of the property has resulted in this pattern. Rich pastoralists were against the partition, for fear of losing rights over pastoral resources in the frankincense-growing areas. They presumed that exploitation of frankincense would prove anathema to herding. Those with less vested interests in pastoralism, on the other hand, were in favour of the intensive exploitation and partition of the resource. These were mostly herd-poor collecting families and some traders based in the villages. The impact of this is currently felt by the descendants of the pastoral faction who do not own sufficient stock to practise herding as their ancestors did, and are therefore obliged to rent or enter share-cropping relations with legitimate holders with inherited rights.

In the northwest agricultural region, some members of land-holding groups did not participate in the initial distribution of land, and opted to practise stock breeding. If those previously pastoral members aspire or are forced to cultivate, they are obliged to loan fields, the same way families with limited herd have loaned milk camels in the pastoral economy. Although close agnates may allow a poor member of an owning family and sometimes a non-owning kinsman, to exploit frankincense freely until a member of the right-holding group requires its use, landless tenants are generally not loaned the property. Quite commonly they enter rental or share-cropping relations with right-holding kinsmen.

Unbalanced economic relations between the actual collectors and other groups involved in the production of frankincense, have been a marked feature of the sector. Prior to the 1969 revolution which introduced a sustained cooperative model of development, a traditional tri-partite system of distribution was most common. It dictated that the gross value of the seasonal produce of the joint unit of production be partitioned into three equal shares. One part was allocated to right-holders for access to the property, another went to the local traders as compensation for the joint expenditure obtained by the work party partly in the form of credit. The remaining portion was all that was left for the landless gatherers and their families. Wage labour (which was sometimes paid in kind) and a rental arrangement, albeit the former to a limited extent, were and still are the other major forms of socioeconomic exploitation.

Partly because local traders represented an economic group distinct from incense collectors in rural areas and partly because the interaction between traders and collectors was frequent and of most consequence, the latter spoke of their subordinate relations with kin patrons. In one verse, religious actuaries for shop owners and other townspeople were described as an unholy alliance to exploit collectors. Merchants and intermediaries were widely accused of having devised measurement units and bush scales to extort extra unaccounted incense.

Moreover, weights were claimed to have been made heavier to the advantage of traders. Collectors were said to be given on credit shoddy goods and goods that remained in the store for a long time. Thus they were denied, in many cases, good quality goods on credit terms. Merchants who had a monopoly on marketing the produce of their kin client collectors before the latter half of the twentieth century were also accused of deceiving by declaring lower value for the consigned incense merchandise.

It is interesting to note that some of the mechanisms used by local merchants against kin producers are replicas of those Somali traders claim to have experienced in Aden before the 1970s. Merchants in Aden are said to have obliged Somali traders to buy shoddy goods, the same way Somalis obliged kin clients to accept poor quality goods on credit. Merchants in Aden are reported to have dishonestly fiddled measurement units to their advantage, a tendency which local traders are also said to have resorted to. In the light of this, it can be said that local merchants were passing on to their clients the effect of the swindling practices to which they were subjected in Aden.

Many reasons account for the failure of the cooperative movement in the frankincense sector of Somalia. Poet spokesmen for the collectors rightly indict various deductions of substantial magnitude, more than 17%, both in kind and cash, that were deducted from the value of the frankincense which was sold to public enterprise. Deferred payment of the purchased merchanise contributes to the disappointment of the collectors.

The organisation's development record is dismal by all standards. Grandiose promises to bring about social services unknown in the isolated areas of the frankincense production often failed to materialise. Furthermore, to abolish relations of economic exploitation between collectors and local traders proved an elusive goal. The movement also failed to foster some form of collective organisation to supersede the traditional corporate production of frankincense.

Inadequate state credit and lack of a just and effective distribution of the limited facilities further undermined the movement. These facilities were not only insufficient, they were not tuned to the real needs of the collecting families. It is not easy for a modern enterprise to supply constantly, throughout the season, credits as varied as the people's needs for basic subsistence food and daily domestic goods.

These constraining factors tended to reduce the enterprise created to modernise the traditional sector into a lethargic mandatory buying agency. Of most consequence, the enterprise was manipulated by officials for economic ends. Enterprise resources allocated for development were appropriated, and high-level officials also allowed merchants to trade in frankincense, in contravention of the monopoly.

At the local level, elected cooperative leaders, mostly traders, dominated the production of frankincense. As rural intellectuals they acted as intermediaries between government and cooperativised kin producers. They were able to understand, interpret and communicate government decisions to collectors living in their areas of ethnic origin (for information as a source of power in the context of cooperativisation see Guillet 1979:164–169). They escorted government officials in rural areas, they also acted as community spokesmen by elaborating and commenting on some of the stated official views which required further elucidation or stress.

Cooperative leaders who were mainly traders served as a better source of credit than the public enterprise, as noted above. They were able to provide reliable and sustained credit facilities for kin client collectors from shops in the rural villages dominated by particular lineages. Such facilities coincided with the frequent and varying needs of the collectors. For example, if a kin collector becomes insolvent he may be allowed to labour on a running credit.

The failure of the enterprise to attain socioeconomic changes, not to mention its extortionate practices and the domination of the cooperatives by elected middle-men, undermined the movement and reinforced traditional relations of production. As a source of credit the enterprise corresponded to the role of the local merchants who previously provided credits. Cooperative committees, in turn, corresponded to the traditional intermediaries between traders and collectors.

The control of the frankincense export crop which is hard-currency-generating merchandise, and the general disenchantment with the enterprise and its failure to bring about anticipated socioeconomic changes, among other factors, encouraged a pervasive parallel trade.

Paradoxically, cooperative leaders acted as intermediaries for the informal trade by establishing a link between traders and local collectors. Economic grievances, for instance the failure of the enterprise or other state agencies to make essential goods available in some isolated areas, further acted to encourage the informal trade. Exploiting such grievances local traders urged kin producers to sell goods to them, on the pretext that they would import the required goods.

Some traders claim that they were unfairly treated by government officials in terms of obtaining permits for the export of frankincense and other commercial gums. To circumvent this, they urged their kin collectors to sell goods to them illicitly. In this way it was the local people who benefitted from the dealing of frankincense and other valuable community resources.

The pervasive and dynamic role of the informal trade in frankincense is due to the fact that it integrated the interests of the various economic groups. The collectors sold superior grades of *meydi* incense illicitly to the private traders for higher prices. The competition between the enterprise and enterprising traders for superior frankincense had compelled the enterprise to increase producer prices several times during the period of this study. This also meant increased income for collectors from the incense sold to the state enterprise. District and regional officials who are responsible for control of the parallel trade, turned a blind eye to it for economic ends. And for traders who are strapped for hard currency, export of frankincense earns them the means to import consumer goods which are claimed to profit them more than the exported frankincense.

Given the absence of an effective modern organisation to seek orderly and just transformation, and the need to transform some of the customary means of distribution, right-holders and landless tenants started to manipulate relations of production in ways that are inimical to agnatic solidarity. The most important transformation was the tendency towards a rental arrangement with respect to the commercial forests in lieu of the traditional share-cropping.

In those areas where share-cropping still prevails the owners seem to be forced, by opposition from tenants, to modify the terms of distribution instead of allowing renting which is favourable for the tenants. And where seasonal rent has become the accepted norm, right-holders tend to set exorbitant rates for the exploitation of the commercial frankincense forests. To reduce the amount required to pay in terms of the existing share-cropping, some collectors for their part lower the actual seasonal produce and keep the undeclared amount for themselves.

In Alula district where an attempt was made by the district cooperative leadership to regulate the soaring rent, an imposed modest rate was achieved at the cost of stirring up traditional social schisms between the major lineages living in the district. The numerically dominant group in the district dominated the management of the cooperative, but many of its landless members rented fields that belong to the traditionally aristocratic lineage and its minority allied groups. The latter groups considered rent regulation and other anticipated reforms to be a pretext to undermine customary rights by the dominant group, which was seen to capitalise on the government's socialist policy of equality and social justice. In other districts where rent was not regulated, we witness escalation of rent or a modified form of the traditional share-cropping.

My analysis of the problems of the cooperative movement in the frankincense sector of Somalia indicts inefficiency, corruption and graft as the major impediments in the establishment of an effective modern enterprise. This approach, which was propounded by John S. Saul for the Tanzanian case (in Worsley 1971:347–370), offers a more precise explanation of the actual cause of the failure of the movement in Third World countries than the "traditionalist" views which place the facilitating or constraining factors in the social organisation of these societies (*ibid.*). In the cooperativised frankincense sector of Somalia, the traditional unbalanced relations were perpetuated by graft and corruption on the part of the elected cooperative leaders, enterprise and other government officials.

POSTSCRIPT

Changes that took place after the study

The collapse of the monopoly of the state enterprise and the consequent resurgence of the private sector trade that took place after the defeat of the military regime in February 1991, stands as the most signficant change that took place after this study. This is not a new development and conforms to the past pattern where instituted marketing and credit orgnizations often failed after a short period of time (see chapter one).

The remoteness of the frankincense region and its difficult terrain that disadvantage the frankincense people under normal circumstances in terms of access to public services, proved a blessing in the recent turmoil. Thus, the frankincense region remained relatively less affected by the disruptive, comprehensive and protracted social upheaval in Somalia. This was especially true of the stable Bosaso district. Even in the severly affected Erigavo district, the isloated and mountainous frankincense region acted as a safe refuge and a military strategic position for the Isaaq clans in their struggle against the government forces. However, this led the Gaheyle group in Erigavo district, who claim Majeerteen origin, to be displaced from their frankincense homeland, following the fall of the military government of the same origin.

BIBLIOGRAPHY

Atchley, E. G. 1909, *A history of the use of incense in divine worship*. London: Longmans Green & Co.

Andrzejweski, B. W. 1972, "Poetry in Somali society", in J. B. Pride and J. Holmes (eds.), *Sociolinguistics: selected readings*, pp.252–259. Harmondsworth: Penguin Books.

1985, "Somali literature", in B. W. Andrzejewski, S. Pisazewocz and W. Tylock (eds.), *Literatures in African languages: theoretical issues and sample surveys*, pp. 337–407. Cambridge: Cambridge University Press.

1985, "Oral Literature", in B. W. Andrzejewski, S. Pisazewocz and W. Tylock (eds.), *Literatures in African languages: theoretical issues and sample surveys*, pp. 31–38. Cambridge: Cambridge University Press.

Andrzejweski, B. W. and M. I. Galaal 1963, "A Somali poetic combat", *Journal of African Languages*, 2, Part 1:15–28, 93–100,190–205.

Andrzejweski, B. W. and I. M. Lewis 1964, *Somali poetry: an introduction*. Oxford: The Clarendon Press.

Aronson, D. R. 1980, "Kinsmen and comrades: towards a class analysis of the Somali pastoral sector", *Nomadic Peoples*, No. 7:14–33.

Bergström, T., A. Persson, M. Thulin and A. M. Warfa 1982, "Domestication of frankincense trees. Travel report from the first tour of the project". Unpublished.

Bohannan, P. 1963, "'Land', 'tenure' and 'land-tenure', in D. Biebuyck (ed.), *African agrarian systems*. London: Oxford University Press, pp. 101–111.

Birdwood, G. 1870, "On the genus Boswellia, with descriptions and figures of three new species", *Trans. Linn. Soc. Lond.*, 27:111–148.

Caponera, A. D. 1954, "Water laws in muslim countries". *FAO Development Paper*, No. 43, Agriculture. Rome.

Carter, H. J. 1847, "A description of the frankincense tree of Arabia, with remarks on the misplacement of the 'Libanophorous Region'", in "Ptolemy's Geography", *Journ. Bombay Br. Roy. Asiat. Soc.*, 2:380–390.

Cassanelli, Lee V. 1982, *The shaping of Somali society: reconstructing the history of a pastoral people, 1600–1900*. Philadelphia: University of Pennsylvania.

Coulter, J. 1987, "Market study for frankincense and myrrh from Somalia". Consultancy report to the Government of Somalia. Tropical Development and Research Institute, London.

Drake-Brockman, R. E. 1912, *British Somaliland*. London: Hurst and Blacket.

Ducaale, C. C. 1984, *Taarikhda Beeraha ee Gobollada Wogooyi–Galbeed iyo Awdal*. Xamar (Mogadishu) iyo Hargeysa: Akademiyada Cilmiga Fanka iyo Suugaanta.

Durrill, W. K. 1986, "Atrocious misery: the African origins of famine in northern Somalia, 1839–1884", *American Historical Review*, 91(2):287–306.

Frazer, J. 1957, *The golden bough III: a study in magic and religion*. London: Macmillan and Co. Ltd.

Gavin, R. J. 1977, *Aden under British rule*. New York: Harper & Row Publishers Inc.

Gell, A., 1977, "Magic, perfume, dream", in I. M. Lewis (ed.), *Symbols and sentiments: cross cultural studies in symbolism*, pp.25–38. London: Academic Press.

Gluckman, M. 1943, "Essays on Lozi land and royal property". *Rhodes-Livingstone papers*, No. 10. Rhodes- Livingstone Institute.

Groom, N. 1981, *Frankincense and myrrh: a study of the Arabian incence trade*. Rome and London: Longman Group Limited.

Guidotti, R. 1930, "L'incenso nella Migiurtinia", *L'Agricolt. Colon.*, 24:530–544.

Guillet, D. 1979, *Agrarian reform and peasant economy in southern Peru*. Colombia: University of Missouri Press.

Hepper, N. 1969, "Arabian and African frankincense trees", *Journ. Egypt. Archaeol.*, 55:66–72.

Haakonson, J. M. 1984, *Scientific socialism and self reliance*. Bergen studies in Social Antropology 34. Bergen: University of Bergen.

Henrikson, K. H. 1968, "Report on production and marketing of gums and resins in Somalia". Consultancy report produced for the Goverment of the Somali Republic. Frankfurt am Main.

Hersi, A. A. 1977, "The Arab factor in Somali history: the origins and the development of Arab enterprises and cultural influences in the Somali peninsula". Unpublished Ph.D. diss., University of California, Los Angeles.

Jamal, V. 1987, "Somalia: understanding an unconventional economy", *Development and Change*, 19:203–265.

Johnson, J. W. 1974, *Heelooy Heelooy: the development of the genre Heello in modern Somali poetry*. Bloomington: Indiana University Press.

Lane, E. W. 1954, *Manners and customs of the modern Egyptians*. London: J. M. Dent & Son Ltd.

Lewis, I. M. 1955–1956, "Sifism in Somaliland" , *Bull. Scho. Oriental and African Studies*, xvii, 1955:581–602; xviii:146–160.

1959, "Clanship and contract in northern Somaliland", *Africa*, xxix:247–293.

1961a, "Force and fission in northern Somali lineage structure", *American Anthropologist*, 63:94–112.

1961b, *A pastoral democracy: a study of pastoralism and politics among the northern Somali of the Horn of Africa*. London: Oxford University Press.

1962a, "Historical aspects of genealogies in northern Somali social structure", *J. Afr. Hist.*, iii:35–45.

1962b, "Lineage continuity and modern commerce in northern Somaliland", in P. Bohannan and G. Dalton (eds.), *Markets in Africa*. Northwestern University Press.

1962c, *Marriage and the family in northern Somaliland*. East African Studies No. 15. Kampala: East African Institute of Social Research.

1963, "Dualism in Somali notions of power", *J. Royal Anthropological Institute*, 93:109–116.

1965a, "Shaikhs and warriors in Somaliland", in G. Dieterlen and M. Fortes (eds.), *African systems of thought*, pp.204–223. London.

1965b, "Problems in the comparative study of unilineal descent", in M. Gluckman and F. Eggan (eds.), *The relevance of models in Social Anthropology*, pp.87–112. London: Tavistock Publications.

1969a, "Spirit possession in northern Somaliland", in J. Beattie and J. Middleton (eds.), *Spirit mediumship and society in Africa*. London: Routledge and Kegan Paul Ltd.

1969b, "From nomadism to cultivation: the expansion of political solidarity'" in P. Kaberry and M. Douglas (eds.), *Man in Africa*, pp.59–78. London.

1975, "The dynamics of nomadism: prospects for sedentarisation and social change", in T. Monod (ed.), *Pastoralism in tropical Africa*. London: Oxford University Press.

1980, "Conformity and contrast in Somali Islam'" in I. M. Lewis (ed.), *Islam in tropical Africa*. London: Oxford University Press.

1981, "Somali Democratic Republic", in B. Szajaowski (ed.), *Marxist governments: a world survey*. London: Macmillan.

1986, *Religion in context: cults and charisma*. Cambridge: Cambridge University Press.

1988, *A modern history of Somalia: nation and state in the Horn of Africa*. Boulder: Westview Press.

Laitin, D. D. and S. S. Samatar 1987, *Somalia: nation in search of a state*. Boulder: Westview Press.

Lawrie, J. 1954, "Frankincense", *Somaliland Journal*, 1(1):26–30.

Miles, S. B. 1872, "On the neighbourhood of Bundar Marayah", *Journal of the Royal Geographical Society*, 42:61–76.

Muller, W. W. 1975, "Notes on the use of frankincense in South Arabia. Proceedings of the 9th Seminar". *Seminar for Arabian Studies*, Vol.6. London.

Peck, E. F. 1937, "Survey of gum trade in Somaliland Protectorate". Unpublished.

Persson, A., M. Thulin and A. M. Warfa 1987, "Domestication of frankincense trees. Progress report from the fourth tour of the project". Unpublished.

Samatar, S. S. 1982, *Oral poetry and Somali nationalism: the case of Sayid Mahammad 'Abdille Hassan*. London: Cambridge University Press.

Schoff, W. E. 1912, *The periplus of the Erythraean Sea* (trans. and commentary). New York: Longman.

Swift, J. 1979, "The development of livestock trading in nomad pastoral economy: the Somali case", in L'Equipe ecologie et anthropologie des societes pastorales (ed.), *Pastoral production and society*. Cambridge: Cambridge University Press.

Thulin, M. and A. M. Warfa 1987, "The frankincense trees (Boswellia spp., Burseraceae) of northern Somalia and southern Arabia", *Kew Bulletin*, Vol. 42(3):487–500.

Thulin, M. and P. Claeson 1991, "The botanical origin of scented myrrh (bissabol or habak hadi)", *Economic Botany*, 45(4):487–494.

United Nations Technical Assistance Prcgramme 1952, "The trust territory of Somaliland under Italian administration". New York.

Worsley, P. (ed.) 1971, *Two blades of grass: rural cooperatives in agricultural modernisation*. Papers presented at a conference held at the University of Sussex, Manchester. Manchester: Manchester University Press.

APPENDIX

Somali texts of the translated poems in the study

1
Taariikhda boqollaal kun oo beri fogaa joogta
Bilaad Bunta waagaan aheyn baradii kheryaadka
Boqorrada fircoonkaa arliga baawar ku lahaaye
baalgoraydey gadan jireen meydi noo baxaye
Baayacmushtari kama horeyn beeyada iyo fooxa
Annagaa bilownaye khalquigu biica ma agoone
Berigaa an tilmaamey iyo watqtiga beeshayadu guurto
Ma bedeline dhaquankii horaan weli ku baaqaaye

2
Isku Daalney oo isku dacasney
Marka daartiyo doonyaha u meer

3
Allow carabtii cadcadeyd ee cancanjuuleyd, canbar kuu saar
Aaney ku celcelin

4
Dadka kale carruurtuu dhaluu cadan u dhoofshaaye
Ciida-gale nimaan geel laheyn waa cirka u tuure

5
Idinbasa awrkey dhashiyo aarankey wadatey
Asaxaabihii horeba wey ku intifaaceene
Aahkiro nimaan geel laheyn lama amaaneyne
maxaan idinla awlaadsadaa awgayow awrba maan rarane

6
Geel an naga gablomeyn
Haliba gaawa leedahey
An biyo loo garsaareyn
Gaajana looga yaabeyn
Yaa gubanka noogu yaal

7
Qarkaan meerey qomorkaan galey qaarad waxan gaarey
Habeen qaarkii qoloflaha harruur qararableyntiisa
Qartartaa wixii aan ku jiro oo unaxa qariyaaba
Goortaan u soo qaraxtiro ayey qol ku gurtaaniine
Kii qaadey kii qeybiyey iyo qaarka mid u jooga
Qaayimaddii duubneyd haddii qalinka loo geeyey
Qaariga waddaad ahi hadduu qararabta u dhiibey

Waxan qaadey sagaal qoorqab bey geyb u noqotaaye
Dhagax qoofil ah kalax qoob ah iyo qorigu noo dheere
Kana qadhmuuni qaadaali iyo quluble reeroode
Ninba qeybtii waa kaa haya quruxda xoolaha
Illaahow ma qabad baan nahey qolona aan sheegan
Illaahow waxad noo qortey iyo geybtayadii meedey
Allahayow qasmiga waad taqaan qeybahaan rabo
qadarkii illaah ila damcey iyo geyb ma diidani

8

Cirka da'ay daruuraha onkodey cood ma daaqsado
daalaca ma saaro oo harruur iima soo dego
Seedow dukaan iima yaal dunida suudaan
Deyn kaama qabo la isku diro col iyo duulaan
Weelkeyga ii daa adduun dalab rid weeyaane

9

Wiilyohow magaalada fadhiyey ha i masqaradeyn
Kimis moofo laga soo baxshey oo maxwaj loo yeeley
Adba maanguuraad cuntaa maalin oo idile
Waxa feeraheygii makiney mira fir fiiraaye
Madxin nimaan laheyn geedku waa u mira cawaageede
Waqan maanta dabadeed la arag meel u joogaba e

10

Dhammow saalaxow xaajadaan kuu dhibrinayaaye
Dhallinyaro ka weynaadey iyo dhaaodnkii hore
Dhaantada intaan tumi lahaa facu i dhaafsiiye
Garku nimu dhammeeyaan ahey oo aan dherer u laabneyne
Ma anaa gabdhaha ila dhashey iyo Dhuda-yar ceebeysta
Wax intaan u dhimo ma anigaa dhereran foolkooda
Abaarahakan dhacey aadamuhu wada dhurwaayowye
Meeshii dheecaan lehba naftaa loola dhacayaaye
Dhir la fuulo dhidid howleh iyo dhib iyo tiiraanyo
Beeyada timaha kage dhagta ee aan la iska dhowreynin
Waa dhaafi doonaan haddey dhererg helaaniine
Illaahow arsaaq dhaanta sii kama dhawaadeene

11

Ma gudbo oo garkaa iyo ma tago guda Nugaaleede
Geedaha ma daaqo oo biyaha waa ka garanuuge
Meeshii gasooruhu ka da'ac uma garqaadiine
Godka Lumanka, golihii Indhacad, gagada Hoohaale
Gaax lagama waayoo beryuu godolmaceeyaaye
Waxa la goorgooiyaa goor iyo ayaane
Ginigaa cas maahee ma jiro ganac la siistaaye
Illaahow ha iga goyn geedku waa guunyadeydiiye

12

Geelayaga ma sheegaa
Ma sheegaa shalalax siiyaa
Waa rimeyda boyga leh
Buuraha ku taal
Lambarku beerka kaga yaal

13
Maro waa idlaataa
Maalkuna waa dhanmaadaa
Marso aan gabloomeyn iyo
Meydi baanu leenahey

14
Xumey beeyoy
Xagaagii bey
Xoolo tahayoo
Xudh la siistaa

15
Marka xagaa bilowdaa
Ee gu'gu naga baqoolo
Ee dadka kale bakhtiyayo
Baa beeyadu hagaagtaa

16
Haddey qararab leedahey
Haddii gubadku duulaayo
Geel dhaley ka xoog roon
Haddaad mar ila soo gaarto

17
Ragga xabagta dhaadheer
Xaga iyo mushaadka leh
ENC kula xisaabtama
Iyo ninka habar xiriir la leh
Ee xoogaaga beeraha
Baabuur la xaw yiri
Xamar lacagta lala tago
Gabadhyahey xariir u eg
Xaqa meydin eegtaan
Iyamaad xigi laheyd

18
Wallee ama maanta deyn baxey
Xaadir intaan ka dowdabey
Dalawa geel ka iibsadey
Ama daalac la ii raac
Oo beeyaba dib uma guran

19
Nin Salaada faqdiirtey
Oo fur wuxuu qabey xuurey
Oo fiidkii nus firfiire
Faruuryaha mar la gaarey
Ar hoy feydu ha joogtee
Gorgor sow na fagte

20
Guunyadaada ha daaqsan
Geed fagaara ha joogsan
Xiji gaadihii weeye
allow nooga gargaar
Hebel gooshiga baawqey
Anse waan guntanaa
Xiji gaadihii weeye
Allow nooga gargaar

21
Anigu raaxa ka quustey
Oo ramaad geela ma maalo
Raaridii Madarkii iyo
Adna raaxa ka quuso

22
Sida ceymadka geela
Oo cidla waaya ku raagey
Qalimaalahey Caarow
Waad ceymad yareysey

23

Mar haddey shinni gaarto
Shinni-gaabey ay gaarto
Shansha-dheere gammaan iyo
Gabar shaaximan mooyee
Shan halaad kuma siisto

24
Kuwa Qaaliga jooga
Ee Qadow geela ku maala
Wey noa quudhsanayaane
Wey na quudidoonaan

25
Kolkey dhawaaqdo
Duunyo caana yareyso
Alla kaniyow ina aabe
Dadka noo wada keen
Hoo Hoo Hoo

26
Nageeyow nin ku waayey
Anba weysha xaraash
Anba wiilka ka roor
Hoo Hoo Hoo

27
Alla ninkaad u samaatooy
Badda nageeye
Siduu doonaba yeel
Hoo Hoo Hoo

Waan ku dhawrilahaayoo
Sidaa kuuma dhibeene
Dhallaan baa wat i sii lahoo
Dhulkaan dhuuni ka dooni

29
Qooryarey gabar mayhid
Oo guur lagaa sugi maayo
Qaalintii Dhafan mayhid
Oo dheys lagaa sugimaayo
Ee dhulkey xoolo galeenoo an ka xoogsaneynaa

30
Shuluqshuluqle shaaruba raglow sharaf haweenaadle
Mar hadduu shareeraha galo oo shey walba ogaado
Wuxu sheelada u lulayaa god u shaleeyaa

31
Weyseyso goortaan isiri bey war igu taabteene
Wardigiyo salaadaan ku girey wahan i dhaatsinye
Faataxada goortaan wadwadey waafi ma aheyne
Halkaan tobanka weela u toley ee wiilasha u qeybshey
Waaxya alla gooyow shaley iga walwaaleene
Waxeygii haddaan hoo la odhan waalid baan ahaye
Waxan idhi wax badan baa u go' ay waayadii hore e
Iminkana wakiilkaan lahaa waan u wacayaaye
Go'yaashii wanaagi lahaa idinku waandaabshey
Wasiir iyo wasiir iyro wasiir wey ka bixiwaaya
Xiniinyuhu wadaan idin noqde waaya manidiina
Wareegtadiina nimankii lahaa wey ka bixiwaaye
Hogta kuugu godey hogor yar iyo haam an soo jaraye
Hangool jabey intaan murmurey kuugu hawlgaleye
Hayaay iyo hayaay qeyladii la is hindiidsiiye
Abkiin intaad nooshihiin cadho la weeraada

32
Xijigaan xagaagii dhaweyd xuurtu igu gaartey
Xijigaan ninkii igu xaqliyo xaaska ku ilaabey
Ilaahow ninkii iga xadow adan xalaal oodan

33
Waagoo bilaabmey oo aan shaqada wada bilaabeyno
Boodaan aadney iyo dhulkii beeyada lahaaye
Bartankeeda goortaan tagney baan argney Beyluule
Geedaa u baxey oo wuxu ku yiri war igu soo boobe
Waxey tiri barwaaqaan qabnaa bala la'aaneede
Kuwaa isoo baxshey oo waxey dhaheen buurta kor u fuule
Beegsey dhaheen waxad ka heli wiilal baashi ahe
Haseyeeshee baahaan qabaa waanan ba'ayaaye
Dab buu balbaliyoo wuxu ku shubey baasta kiila ahe
Beyl buu u saarey oo qaxwaha lagula soo boodye
Goortey barwaaqowdey oo uurku balaxoobey
Beeyaad gurtaan oo idinku shaqaad bilowdeene
Xaggee buurta kaga yaal galihii waan u baxayaaye
Waxan idhi warka an kuu bandhigo bilan walaaleeye
Haddaan boqol ido ah leeyahey oo buurta ku ilaasho
Haddaan gidirka beyga leh dhaqdoo baladka joogaayo
Haddaan baare geel leeyahey oo bidix ku haaneedo
Berri Carab haddii an tago oo dibedda boodboodo
Baabuur sabaax ah iyo haddii an B.M. wadanaayo
Bankiyada adduunyada haddii ay lacagi ii buuxdo
Beeyada haddii an gurto oo Booj u hoyanaayo
Been lama hadlee bilan walaan kuuba bixiyeene
Ardey baab riqiisaan ahey oo heysan boqolaale
Haddii boqorku noo saamaxo oo an balo na sii qaadin
Bishatan haddey le'ato waan wada baxeynaaye
Boosaasaanu qaban iyo walaal barashadeydiiye
Baladada an kuu kala tirshee hore u sii baaci
Gosha moxorka badan bey wadadu kaala sii bixiye
Dhaaraca bannaan buu qalbigu kuugu bogayaaye
Bookhaad u dhici iyo walaal bohololoodkiiye
Babacaa qarkaa kaa ah baa lagaga boodaaye
Bannaan baad u bixi iyo bankii damalka weynaaye
Sheekh baashi ah baa jiifa oo aan cidina baaseyne
Ducada ugu boob sheekha waa looga badiyaaye
Jidka bidixda raac dawgu waa kal baxaayaaye
Balad kaa horeeyaa jira oo ay timiri buuxdaaye
Bilcishaa markad gaarto bey wada bildhaantaaye
Horena ugu bood waxad ku dhici ila barwaaqahe
Caagaaga buuxso adoo socodka biisaaya
Dhicirtaa bannaan bey wadadu kaala sii bixiye
Ha u beydhin gaaladu khamrey kula baryaayaane
Cogada u bood adigoo socodka boobaaya
Biyahaaga fuud xiiqda waa lagu bukoodaaye
Galihii banide saaka bey kala boqooleene
Qafil buuran baa lagu dhiftey oo meel bannaan ma lehe
Sahal iyo Salaad Baashe baa lagu yar beydhaaye
Hablahana middii an bileyn waa ay bireeyaane
Baaley ku moodaan haddii adan bildhaameyne
Midna waa baryaa Sahalna waa kugula boodaaye
Isbukhuuri cadarkaaga waa la isku buufshaaaye
Booj baa u hoya oo hadhow bey u baxayaane
Daba biqley socodka waa la iska baaraaye
Bootaan Cabdaa kuugu filan buuri iyo shaahe
Cismaan baari weeyoo hurdadaad ugu bogeysaaye
Saliimna waa wadaad beydad ah oo inan u baahnaaye
Badaha uma dhaco ee oogaduu biis ku leeyahaye
Mataan balaqabeenaa jira aan kaaba baxaheyne
Sahalna waa burcade yuu habeen biixi kaa jabine

Baro iyo Bannaan laguma oga booska Booj yahaye
Barwaaqada adduun baa ku dhane balada ha u yeeran

34
Baalahakan Booj bey habluhu badi u joogaane
Been lama hadlee weyakaa wada barseynaaya
Dhallintuna burdaha waa naqdaa Bara iyo Yaasiine
Dhallinyarada biidka ahi nooma soo bixine
Bashaar gobaadley haddaad booqashada keentey
Bootaan Cabdaa kugu bireyn Booj haddaad timiye
Marka waad boqoolin ee dhabada beeg iskugu taag
Ma Billa oo Siciid waa buktaan ee haba u soo beyrin
Ceel-dibir biyuu leeyahey ee ba'e ku sii meyro
Ragguna waa benderi badow haddaad moodey
Baarafuunka iyo bootarka aad iskugu baahi
Jaamac baa bustaha qaada oo meel bannaan dhiga e
Cabdillaahi baa kugu buteyn bahalka uu heysto
Baalina ha nogon naag xun baa laga bareystaaye

35
Gabaryahey garkaa iyo ka timi guda Nugaaleedka
Gabangoobi lama rooro iyo meel an gacal joogin
Gebi oodan baad soo gashey iyo gawlalo iyo ciine
Gadoobada ma joogaan raggii gaaxsanaan jiraye
Garre iyo haddaad Meyragale gaban i weydiisey
Googarradda sii dhigo wax baad galabsaneysaaye
Iyagaa garneyl weyn haya iyo geed an go'aheyne
Iyagaa gasiin kaaga dhigi kimis an gaafneyne
Garka gudubsan weyakaa ku jira gole habaas weyne
Naa geesna ha u kicin intaa gu'gu ka hooraayo

36
Mahyuubow macnaha gabey haddaad mid iga weydiisey
Anigaa miftaaxa u haya oo mawlaca u sida
Waxan adiga kuu muugan baa ....?
War ma maarantaa yaan qunbulad kugu madoobeyne

37
Cabdiyow micnaha gabey haddaad mid iga weydiisey
Anigaa miftaaxa u haya oo mawlaca u sida
Minshaar xadiid ah iyo afkaan muus ku leeyahey
Shisheeyuhu hadduu muukhdo baan mahadō reebaaye
War ma maarantaa yaan qunbulad kugu madoobeyne

38
Haddii ad garaad leedahey oo ay garasho kuu raacdo
Madaxaaga goobaha leh baad wax u gleysaaye
Haddii kale gashaantaad tahey iyo reera gabadhoode
Guudkaa laguu dabi intaad helin gayaankaaye
Geedkaaga anigaa leh oo geela kaa bixine

39
Afarta irgimood ninkii oodey baan ahaye
Afareyda gabeyga ah ninkii aakidaan ahaye
Afar kii yaqaan iyo afmaal waa iga oo'osadaye
Adigana aflowow haddaad ibila maashaaye
Waa kuu afxumo ugaas in ad-erey tiraahdaaye

40
Laga reysey doonyaha ku rida oo ha raacina
Laga reysey rubi kuuma sido reerkuna xumaa
Laga reysey raajicaddii iyo reydalkii Cadmeed
Mid Illaahey soo ridey oo reer wadaa yimide
Waa key miskiinkiyo rabeen reer bustaaliguye
Ku reyreya waa hortii wada rareydeene

41
Xiji daanad weeyee habxumadaan iskaga daayey
Tobanka daalin oo nalagu darey baan iskaga daayey
Anigoo dakaan iyo harraad labadaba u diiqsan
Wiil baa waxaagii duwadey baan iskaga daayey
Dakad iyo dillaal buu go'ay baan iskaga daayey
Inta kaleba duulaan sidiisaad u dirirtaane
Teersada duqowdiyo Addoosh baan iskaga daayey

42
Addooshow sifnaha gabey nin loo saafo maadihide
Saaxiib baan kula ahaa sano iyo dheeraade
Nin Soomaaliyaa ila tahey oo suuban oo wacane
Ragga saraca waad ila ogtahey suunta uu qabo e
Meel laba subuuc loo maruu uga socdaalaaye
Cidluu seexanaayaa bil iyo laba sagaalaade
Soofkiisa iyo waa huraa siidalkuu dhalaye
Geed sidib ku yaal iyo bob buu sado ka raadshaaye
Wax siyaadso buu leeyahee sidan ma yeeleene
Seedaha wax lagu soo gurey baa subax la keenaaye
Adigana nin sugayaad tahey oo suuqa loo dhigaye
Markii sibidkha lagu daadiyo baad suruq ka eegtaaye
Sonbobadooda rag ad faaqidey oo saabiraa jira e
Saatirkaanu kugu dhaariney iyo suuradaha nebiye
Birimada wax suurta gal ah yaan sii ku leenahay e
Sukundaduna waa sicir dhexe iyo meydi suu yahey e
Teersada ha nagu soo saladin waa siko iyo yaabe

43
Siciidow sifnaha gabey adaa saagac ku ahaaye
Sida u sheegtey labadeenatani waa isla soconaaye
Saaxiibnimaa inoo dhexa iyo sama iyo dheeraade
Ragga saraca waan kula aqaan suunta uu qabo
Aniguba siniin baan ka gurey sidibta Tooxoode
Safar dheer socdaal iyo wixii mawjad nagu seyrmey
Shilin baaba laga siin jirey suuqa Cadan weyne
Isagoo sidaa lagu qabaan saabir ku aheyne
Sukunto iyo Birimo ninkii saahibaa hela
Maxaa kaaga saawa ah haddii teerso laga siisto